BENCHES, STOOLS, AND CHAIRS

A GUIDE TO ERGONOMIC WOVEN SEATING

WALTER TURPENING

AND

DEBORAH HELD

STACKPOLE BOOKS

Essex, Connecticut
Blue Ridge Summit, Pennsylvania

STACKPOLE BOOKS

An imprint of Globe Pequot, the trade division of The Rowman & Littlefield Publishing Group, Inc.
4501 Forbes Blvd., Ste. 200
Lanham, MD 20706
www.rowman.com

Distributed by NATIONAL BOOK NETWORK
800-462-6420

Photography by Walter Turpening, unless otherwise noted; Brandy Clements of the Silver River Center for Chair Caning (credited as SRCCC) took those in the foreword; Jeffrey Sturgill of Sturgill Photographic Arts (credited as SPA) took the cover photo and others as credited.

We have made every effort to ensure the accuracy and completeness of these instructions. We cannot, however, be responsible for human error, typographical mistakes, or variations in individual work.

British Library Cataloguing in Publication Information available

Library of Congress Cataloging-in-Publication Data

Names: Turpening, Walter, 1947– author. | Held, Deborah, 1967– author.
Title: Benches, stools, and chairs : a guide to ergonomic woven seating /
  Walter Turpening, Deborah Held.
Description: First edition. | Lanham, MD : Stackpole Books, an imprint of
  Globe Pequot, the trade division of the Rowman & Littlefield Publishing
  Group, Inc., [2022] | Summary: "The authors teach how to take the
  measurements needed for perfect ergonomic comfort and how to apply them
  to create your perfect seat. With these step-by-step instructions,
  photos, and diagrams, you will see how to custom seating and be able to
  replicate these techniques in your own benches, stools, and chairs"—
  Provided by publisher.
Identifiers: LCCN 2021048582 (print) | LCCN 2021048583 (ebook) | ISBN
  9780811770507 (paperback) | ISBN 9780811770514 (epub)
Subjects: LCSH: Seating (Furniture)—Design and construction. | Chair
  caning—Handbooks, manuals, etc. | Rush-work—Handbooks, manuals, etc. |
  Furniture making—Handbooks, manuals, etc. | Design—Human factors.
Classification: LCC TT197.5.C45 T87 2022 (print) | LCC TT197.5.C45
  (ebook) | DDC 684.1/3—dc23/eng/20211209
LC record available at https://lccn.loc.gov/2021048582
LC ebook record available at https://lccn.loc.gov/2021048583

♾™ The paper used in this publication meets the minimum requirements of American National
Standard for Information Sciences—Permanence of Paper for Printed Library Materials, ANSI/
NISO Z39.48-1992.

First Edition

CONTENTS

ACKNOWLEDGMENTS

First and foremost, to Ellen. I would not be making benches, stools, and chairs if she had not supported me creatively and emotionally. She was frustrated by not finding fabrics in the colors she wanted. I encouraged her to try weaving (I knew nothing about it), and after she took a couple of classes, I gave her her first loom. She encouraged me to try woodworking, and that led to me making a footstool. After many benches in white cord, she said, "You need to add some color." That led to learning about cord braiding, and on to color cord. When I struggled with colors and blending, her artistic eye helped solve the problems. Ellen taught me, day to day, how to observe and use color.

As the business evolved, and along with it the need to travel to shows, Ellen either took care of things at home or came along on the long drives (even though she disliked long road trips). We made them into fun adventures.

Together we were more than each of us could have been alone.

My brother, Roger. Together we supported each other all our lives, through thick and thin, and during many of each other's screwball projects.

David Guy, a friend for twenty years, who helped in the shop, making benches and chairs, and at numerous shows with preparations, travel, and setup and take down. Our weekly breakfasts were important discussions on directions to take.

The members of the Contemporary Handweavers of Houston and the Contemporary Handweavers of Texas. Thank you for your support during the many years we were members. The list is long, and those who have one of the early benches know who you are. You helped me immensely to develop a comfortable bench for weaving and spinning. Thank you.

The Overmountain Weaver's Guild and the Western North Carolina Handweavers Guild, who accepted Ellen and me and encouraged us.

To all the customers who have become friends and have given me ideas.

Jeff Sturgill, who helped early on and for more than twenty years, so that I could have professional photographs for brochures and promotions. A friend.

Lisa Guy Castle, owner of Wrap-It-Mail, who custom boxed and shipped all of my pieces for nearly twenty years. A friend.

Thanks to Tim Callaway for selling me cord braiders, as well as mentoring me on them and on cord-making processes.

Last but not least, Debbie Held, who had the idea to write an article for *Spin Off* magazine (2019). Then she agreed to coauthor this book. Without her, this book would never have made it past an idea in 2020. She added many ideas and provided the skills needed to make my technical writing readable for the common person. It was quite a leap for both of us.

—Walt Turpening
July 2021

Ellen Turpening at Maryland Sheep and Wool Festival, 2015. JAY PULLI

To my son, Beck, who encouraged me to try once again and then cheered when I succeeded. You inspire me every day.

My parents, whose lead I only hope to follow. Growing older with them has been my life's great and unexpected reward.

My brothers, for lessons learned and loyalty. One, the loving companion of my youth; the other, a stalwart reflection of where we come from.

My bestie, Margie, for remembering who I was and knowing who I can still be. It's only through your patient example that I have learned to be a friend.

And to Walt Turpening, for his gracious invitation to help share this vision. With great patience and trust, you let me be exactly who I am. I have grown so very much from this process, and I thank you.

Were it not for the help and support of a handful of generous friends, my career change from one-time business writer to writer of spinning content could not have happened. Special thanks to Kim Carr, for keeping me in stitches and loaning me that spindle; sweet Clara, for making it all possible; Lynn, for sharing (especially Stanley); and Spinnifer, for the near-daily fiber chat, laughter, and truths.

And Kim Berendt, for tirelessly telling me that I could . . . until I did.

Learning to spin, and the members of the handspinning and fiber community I have met both online and in person, have changed the course of my life for the better.

Finally, Walt and I both thank our editor, Candi Derr, and the folks at Stackpole Books, for this experience.

With gratitude,

—Deborah Held
July 2021

FOREWORD

"Chair caning" and "wicker" are umbrella terms for many types of woven seats, including cane, rush, splint, Shaker tape, and Danish cord weaving. The craft dates to ancient Egypt and China, bounced around the globe with colonization, experienced a resurgence in the mid-twentieth century (especially in Scandinavia), and is currently very trendy worldwide in the twenty-first century. Chair-seat weaving is rooted in geometry, botany, physics, world history, economics, and design. The variety of materials and patterns that can be used are innumerable. Though the traditional craft has largely remained the same for millennia, innovations occurred throughout history, in the typical time periods of the Industrial Revolution and, out of necessity, the First and Second World Wars, when embargoes on rattan and shipping trade issues were common. After working on thousands of chairs, and studying thousands more, one thing is for certain: Chairs never cease to surprise me with the variations in weaving patterns, materials, and construction elements.

Corded chairs include paper rush (Photo 1) and Danish cord (Photo 2) or any plant fibers woven or twisted and wrapped around the rails. Cords can be either harvested grasses twisted together or manufactured, pre-twisted cords (made from grasses and/or paper materials). Although the plants grow in watery areas across the United States, the harvesting process is so labor intensive that few chair weavers in this country work with authentic rushes and instead opt for manufactured versions such as twisted Kraft paper and two-ply twill seagrass cord, sometimes called Hong Kong Grass.

Photo 1. Rush-woven chair. 33″ H x 18.5″ W x 17″ D; seat height: 16″. srccc

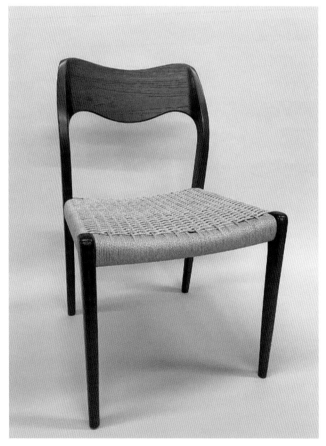

Photo 2. Danish cord-woven chair. 31.5″ H x 19.5″ W x 17″ D; seat height: 18″. srccc

Photo 3. Hickory splint-woven chair. 33.25″ H x 17″ W x 13.5″ D; seat height: 16.5″. srccc

Photo 4. Shaker tape-woven chair. 33.5″ H x 18″ W x 14″ D; seat height: 18″. srccc

Other chair seats woven in a warp/weft method are made of splint reed, oak splints, or hickory bark (Photo 3), and Shaker tape (Photo 4) in a variety of patterns.

Walter Turpening's designs came about organically but with no small amount of refining and scrutiny of function. He elevated his designs beyond function and ergonomics by adding color and intricate weaving patterns based on textile weaving. He created a bridge between textile craft and seat weaving, the likes of which are rare even among the contemporary craft movement.

Walt's chairs, benches, and stools can be woven in an infinite number of pattern and color combinations. The corded seats were inspired by his wife Ellen's loom-weaving practice, and the two of them collaborated on the original designs and ergonomic construction of the frame itself, paying attention to the sitter as well as the aesthetic construction of the chair. Sitting for long periods of time causes serious postural and health issues. Loom weavers and spinners sit for long stretches, immersed in their craft. Walter created a frame designed to address the blood flow and postural issues that result from long-term sitting at the loom or the spinning wheel. He has engineered his own modified versions of loom-weaving tools to assist with his seat-weaving process, which he shares with his students in his sold-out in-person workshops.

Contemporary furniture makers who employ woven seating in their designs most often rely on historically inspired materials and weaving patterns. Few studio makers have gone the extra mile to innovate both the frame and the woven seat. In the case of Walter's designs, the woven seat is the point of focus—indeed, it's a "wow" factor. Textile weavers, spinners, and other artists covet these seats, and his wait list for both classes and commissions has extended a year or more since inception.

Having woven a spinner's bench (which can also be used as a dressing bench for my looms) in one of Walter's classes, I'm very excited about this book. In fact, each person in the class was excited about the prospect of weaving other patterns on other benches. I wove the advancing point twill pattern in neutral colors, but I can't wait to weave the diamond twill and use graded colors on my next seat. As once is never enough to be an expert weaver, I am thrilled for this book so that I can continue to progress through patterns and color combinations on my own time and/or at home while listening to a podcast. The process is accessible, meditative, and enjoyable with comfy and attractive results.

—Brandy Clements

INTRODUCTION

Duke Hwan of Khi,
First in his dynasty,
Sat under his canopy
Reading his philosophy;
And Phien the wheelwright
Was out in the yard
Making a wheel.
Phien laid aside
Hammer and chisel,
Climbed the steps,
And said to Duke Hwan:
"May I ask you, Lord,
What is this you are reading?"
The Duke said:
"The experts, The authorities."
And Phien asked:
"Alive or dead?"
"Dead a long time."
"Then," said the wheelwright,
"You are reading only
The dirt they left behind."
Then the Duke replied:
"What do you know about it?

You are only a wheelwright.
You had better give me a good explanation
Or else you must die." The wheelwright said:
"Let us look at the affair
From my point of view.
When I make wheels
If I go easy, they fall apart,
If I am too rough, they do not fit.
If I am neither too easy nor too violent
They come out right. The work is what
I want it to be.
You cannot put this into words:
You just have to know how it is.
I cannot even tell my own son exactly how it is done,
And my own son cannot learn it from me.
So here I am, seventy years old,
Still making wheels!
The men of old
Took all they really knew
With them to the grave.
And so, Lord, what you are reading there
Is only the dirt they left behind them."[1]

This book is, at best, some dirt about the woven benches, stools, and chairs I've developed and made for customers over the past nearly thirty years. Some aspects are how I worked to make the frames, some are of making custom-colored braided cord, and still others are how the seats and seat backs themselves are woven. Some shop machinery is used to do the basic woodworking for the frames themselves, but hand tools are used for the frames' final shaping and finishing. As for the woven fabric, commercial braiders are used to make the cotton cord relatively quickly and in volume. However, all seat and seat back weaving is done by hand. In my in-person Weave-a-Bench workshops, students learn those hands-on lessons I cannot put into words, by experience and by touch. Sure, some lessons can be taught through precise drawings and by explanation, but other lessons, including checking the legs of a seat for straightness and/or wrapping the warp

onto the frame with just the right amount of tension, can only be mastered through the experience of touch. How to tension and stretch each warp cord just enough is felt through the fingertips, and the final determination of appropriate tension is made by having the students close their eyes and gently strum each cord, the same way one would strum a guitar—listening to and feeling the sound of each. My goal with this book is to share my own journey to seat making as my second career, as well as the supplies and detailed instructions needed to closely replicate or riff off the spinner's chairs, weaving benches, rockers, stools, and the like I've been making for the past twenty-five years.

"Benches, Stools & Chairs," the business tagline, came about following the progression of my development as a woodworker. The initial design was a solution to a bad old footstool inherited along with my dad's rocking chair. The footstool was a box with legs, with tufted

---

1. "Duke Hwan and the Wheelwright" from *The Way of Chuang Tzu*, translated by Thomas Merton (Boston: Shambhala Library, 2004), 92–94.

leather and horsehair padding. Its biggest problem was instability—the stool toppled over when scooted on the floor. When a weaver friend sat on the updated stool, she asked whether I would make a larger one for her loom, which she would use as a bench. The innovation process then began, which was sometime in 1993. Over the next few years working as a hobbyist, I learned a lot about the ergonomics of people and the dimensions of handweaving looms. Just as important, I realized, was learning about actual seat weaving, commercially braided cotton cord and where to source it, and woodworking methods and frame designs, which together would help me achieve an inherently comfortable seat.

I made a couple of solid wood stools, which instead ended up as nice tables. Their edges were the real problem, and where the discomfort started, as these edges

Photo 5. Leg rest; walnut and cherry. 16″ H x 12″ D x 18″ W.

Photo 6. Ellen's weaving bench; maple and walnut. 21″ H x 13″ D x 24″ W.

pressed into the back of the user's legs. Around this same time, I gave Ellen what became her dream handloom, so I experimented by making her a solid wood bench, as was the fashion, to use with it.

While living in Houston in 1992, Ellen and I went on a driving vacation to the southern Appalachians. During this trip we visited various craft schools and studios, where I was introduced to seats woven with the traditional materials such as cane, rush, hickory splints, Shaker tape, and more. At one of the shops, I bought the book *The Craft of Chair Seat Weaving*, by George Sterns. I noticed here and from other weaving-bench inspiration that they were all being made with a relatively flat seat surface.

By this point Ellen had been a weaver for about ten years and was a member of the Contemporary Handweavers of Houston, so I was familiar with weaving materials and methods. I played with the idea of a simple frame with a woven seat made from rug-weaving materials and techniques, which is how I learned the nuances of using weaving tension to create a firm but giving seat surface. I also learned that trying to create a loom-style fabric with typical seat-weaving materials took an awfully long time

to produce. Not only that, but these basic materials also made a stiff seat. To top it off, these items weren't easily available in Houston anyway. On a lark, I visited my local hardware store, where I bought white ⅛-inch cord, both plied and braided, and began experimenting with weaving this cord onto the seat frame.

At the same time I was thinking about how to make a more stable leg/foot rest. The problem of the old box design from my dad's day was that the center of mass was high and the footprint was smaller than the top. Any attempt to push/slide the stool easily caused it to tip over as its feet caught on the floor.

As members of the Contemporary Handweavers of Houston, the weaving and spinning community was important to both Ellen and me. For her, it provided encouragement while she learned to weave. For me, not only did I come to love the art of weaving, but the members also offered feedback on my work as they used their traditional-style benches at their various looms. The spinners in the group helped, too, giving me insight into how to make seating for them at their spinning wheels, which turned out to be just as diverse as looms!

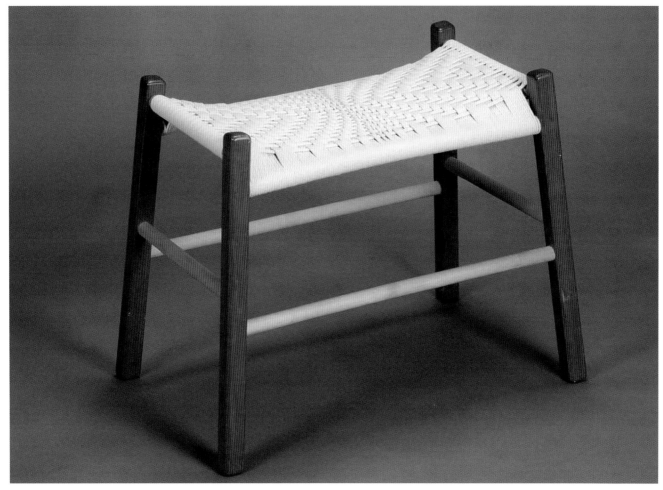

Photo 7. Weaving bench; mahogany and maple; with white commercial cotton cord seat. 21″ H x 13″ D x 24″ W.

During this time, it became clear that the adage "form follows function" described my thoughts on making seating. Seating, for whatever purpose, must fit the person using it and be customized to position them comfortably at their loom, spinning wheel, dining table, or desk. This is why all my seating designs are made to order, so as to fit the person and the particular function it will be used for in their home or business. The simple equations I use for determining fit are scalable for all people and all their seating needs.

The guiding principles to developing the designs are (1) fit the person, (2) position them to work comfortably, and (3) make the final product pleasing to the eye. The first requires knowing up to five different body measurements (as each of us is unique); the second requires knowing the task, purpose, or primary use of the seat; and the third is the blending of wood, cord, and the desires of the customer.

In some traditional chair designs (for example, the Windsor chair), it's the splayed legs that make the chair stable, and so I built upon this idea. I found that combining the frame for weaving with the splayed legs created the trapezoidal-shaped seat and seat back that you will see featured throughout this book. Using cord for the weaving of the seat, it became clear that the front edge of the seat was still a problem, as here again it cut or pressed into the back of the legs. The idea of positioning the front and back seat rails lower than the side rails came to mind, as this would yield a woven but lightly curved surface, allowing the user's legs to rest against the cording instead of the wooden rails. And thus a successful leg rest for Dad's rocker was finally born, as was one of the main design elements for my line of ergonomic seats.

Ellen's weaving study group met at our house periodically, and during one gathering a member sat on the now-updated leg rest. As I was walking by, she asked me, "Can you make one of these for me to use at my loom?" And thus began the journey. We worked out basic dimensions, and a bench was made. Showing it at our weaving guild meeting resulted in others asking to place their own orders. Some of the guild members are still using their benches and chairs all these years later.

WT Logo

In 1993, people began asking for a signature on their benches, so I turned to my collection of books by and about well-known woodworkers to find more information on the topic. I found that each person had their own recognizable style. However, each also dated and signed or branded their work. Generally, this was done in out-of-sight places and was usually the maker's signature. My

Photo 8. WT brand, 1⅛″ W.

bench design was evolving in such a way that there was no out-of-the-way place to leave my mark, so it would be visible. I decided to take my monogram, which I'd been using to mark books I wanted to keep, and to fashion it as a branding iron. I took three weeks of a silversmithing class to learn silver soldering and used hard brass to bend and solder a simple brand. I used it for more than twenty-five years, heating the branding iron with a propane torch before each use, until it finally broke and I had a "proper" branding iron made.

The brand is burned into the right rear leg of all the benches, stools, and chairs that I make.

As business increased, my friend Dave would come by to help with various aspects of the woodworking. In time, he learned to cut all the parts needed for as many as five or six benches or chairs, which sped up the work process. For those pieces, I added a single dot above the logo. Dave eventually learned the techniques of shaping, and on a few benches and chairs he worked all the way to final glue-up. For these, the logo has two dots above it. I have always done the weaving myself.

As a woodworker, as in any craft, we begin with a few skills and ideas. Some may be purely practical, such as building a box in which to store your stuff. As our skills improve, we may experience the work and viewpoints of other makers through classes or workshops. This exposure inspires new ideas, which leads to learning more skills, which then triggers more ideas. This is part of the creative cycle.

During my career in geophysics, I found that being out in the field collecting data, going back to the office and processing the data, and then getting back out in the field with different, newly found approaches helped me uncover the answers to most of the problems I was tasked to solve. Even more important was interacting with those in related sciences and technologies, and then applying their approaches in different ways. Later, when I was managing from an office, I lost interest in my corporate career. This is when my woodworking hobby helped me become a more creative person.

This hobby started when Ellen suggested that I needed more in my life than working on cars—my first real hobby and the one that, coincidentally, led to our meeting. So I took an evening adult-education class in stack lamination and wood-furniture design at a local vocational school. The class was taught by Frank Flynn, a Pittsburgh furniture maker. In the class, slabs/planks/blocks were glued into rough shapes and then "sculpted" into freeform-shape furniture using gouges and mallets, rasps, sanders, and so forth. Initially, the exercises were making small hand sculptures intended to teach hand-friendly shapes—pieces that, by their looks, invited a person to pick them up and fondle them. This practice taught me careful hand-tool use. Frank taught his students that they needed to learn how to cut wood by hand and that they should learn to respect the materials. Along the way you would learn the wood's limits and to respect those, too. This has always stuck with me. A second class with Frank on traditional joinery techniques further taught respect for different species of wood and their use in making furniture.

It is my hope that this collection of my own experiences and lessons gained in seat making will be of use to hobby woodworkers and professional furniture makers alike. While my beloved Ellen is no longer here with us, I do believe that she'd be delighted by this latest endeavor.

ARE YOU SITTING COMFORTABLY?

How comfortable are you while seated at your weaving loom, your spinning wheel, or even your countertop or desk? Odds are, not very, and that's because sitting for any length of time in nearly any commercially available seat or chair is one of the worst things a person can do to their spine, hips, neck, and shoulders.

The more time we spend seated, the worse the pain and the damage can become. The spine and neck can compress, causing disc and muscle degeneration, while a hard, unyielding seat puts undue pressure on the hips. Changing up the seat's material to one that is woven to cradle and support the body's full weight is one means of thwarting this type of damage, as I've discovered through numerous iterations of my hand-built, handwoven benches and chairs. I am also careful to measure my customers in a way that allows me to custom-build a seat best suited for their purpose and their person. These measurements, along with a simple mathematical equation, make for a completely scalable way for anyone to experience what it means to be sitting comfortably at their loom or wheel, in their at-home workspace, or while knitting or stitching in their own Knitter's Rocker.

At Your Weaving Loom

WEAVING DYNAMICS

Though rhythmic and meditative, weaving is also a physically engaging and dynamic activity. Three actions occur fluidly and repetitively while the weaver is seated at the loom: (1) pressing down on the foot treadles, which raises the warp threads, creating shed; (2) "throwing" the weft shuttle through this open shed; and (3) gripping and pulling in the beater bar, to beat the weft into place.

If you're a weaver, you know that treadling requires lower body power to lift up and hold the shafts in place while you throw the shuttle and beat the weft. If you are not comfortably positioned, this process can cause strain to your knees, hips, and lower back.

Throwing the shuttle back and forth requires you to move your arms freely across the width of your warp, while almost simultaneously reaching for the beater bar and pulling it in. Improper body positioning can strain the muscles in your shoulders and lower neck when you lift your arms up and onto the breast beam each time you beat the weft.

At the loom, your body's range of motion is dependent on your loom bench—particularly the height of its seat and how this positions you at your loom. I rely on four simple, key measurements: lower leg length, elbow height, treadle height, and breast beam height, which I then calculate to determine an optimal bench seat height. This is the same formula and worksheet that I've been using with my customers and sharing with my students for the past twenty years.

DETERMINING YOUR BEST WEAVING BENCH HEIGHT

Your Body Measurements

For the most accurate results in taking the measurements for any of the custom seats in this book, I recommend using a yardstick or a sturdy tape measure instead of the flexible cloth tape used by those who sew. You will also need to recruit a friend who can lend a helping, steady hand.

LOWER LEG LENGTH (LLL)

While standing barefoot or in the footwear you'd normally wear while weaving, measure the number of inches from the floor up to the back of both knees, where the crease develops at the bend. Usually, this range is 16–19 inches. If one leg is shorter than the other, use the longer measurement.

ELBOW HEIGHT (EH)

While sitting on a hard surface (such as your current loom bench), relaxed but not slouching, hold your forearm horizontal with your upper arm vertical, making a 90-degree angle. Measure from the bottom of your elbow to the top of the seat. This range is usually 8–12 inches. Repeat with the other arm. If these measurements differ, use the shorter measurement.

Your Loom Measurements

TREADLE HEIGHT (TH)

This measurement redefines where the floor is while weaving. While sitting at your loom, place your feet on the treadles as you would while weaving. Note where the ball of your foot rests on the treadle. Measure from that point, under your foot on top of the treadle, down to the floor. For most jack looms with the treadles hinged at the front of the loom, this number ranges from 3 to 5 inches. For other looms (counterbalanced or countermarch) with treadles hinged at the back of the loom, this number ranges from 5 to 11 inches.

BREAST BEAM HEIGHT (BBH)

Measure from the top of the breast beam down to the floor.

Bench Calculations

UPPER TORSO BENCH HEIGHT (UTBH)

Here we are calculating the seat height needed to reposition your elbows to the top of the breast beam:
Breast Beam Height minus Elbow Height (BBH – EH = UTBH)

OTHER CONSIDERATIONS

Most benches available from loom manufacturers have wood plank seats, ¾–1 inch thick, with sharp or slightly rounded front edges. These harsh edges can cause pressure on the back of your thighs when you weave for extended periods at the loom, leading to pain and numbness in your buttocks and legs. Sitting on a hard, flat seat can do the same, and it can also cause damage to your hips and spine. Using sheepskins or other padding to make your bench more comfortable doesn't usually help. This is why the front edges of all my seat frames, and even my footrests, are rounded with a ½-inch curve, so as not to press into the back of the legs. Should you decide to add padding for your own reasons, be sure to factor in its thickness when calculating your bench height.

If the difference between the upper and lower torso bench heights is more than 2 inches (as in the case of taller looms in which the breast beam height is more than 32 inches) and/or a person has an elbow height less than 9 inches in addition to longer legs (over 18 inches), a thicker padding such as a closed cell foam of 1–1 ½ inches thick is needed to boost the weaver's elbow height for easier beating of the weft. Round the seat edge as suggested and extend the padding around this edge. (This is one of the reasons I designed the curved woven seat bench and use 1-inch dowels for the seat rails. The design allows a greater curve to be made.)

LOWER TORSO BENCH HEIGHT (LTBH)

Here we are calculating the bench height required to have your knees level with your hips when you begin pushing on the treadles:

Lower Leg Length plus Treadle Height (LLL + TH = LTBH)

Sample Calculation A

BBH = 30 inches
EH = 9 inches
Upper Torso Bench Height (BBH – EH) = 21 inches
LLL = 18.5 inches
TH = 3.5 inches
Lower Torso Bench Height (LLL + TH) = 22 inches
Bench Height A = 22 inches

Sample Calculation B

BBH = 34 inches
EH = 8.5 inches
Upper Torso Bench Height (BBH – EH) = 25.5 inches
LLL = 18 inches
TH = 6 inches
Lower Torso Bench Height (LLL + TH) = 24 inches
Bench Height B = 25.5 inches

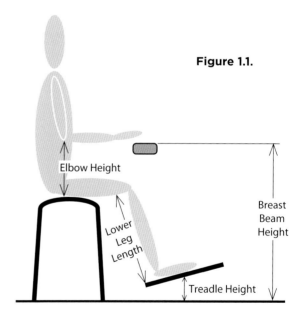

Figure 1.1.

Elbow Height

Breast Beam Height

Lower Leg Length

Treadle Height

Your elbows are at the top of the breast beam and clear it as you throw the shuttle and reach for the beater bar. Your knees are below your hips when you start to treadle, minimizing the strain on your lower back.

Choose the higher of the two calculations so that your knees are at the same level as your hips and your elbows clear the breast beam. This goes for those weavers with more than one loom and those whose lower leg length measurements differ enough to impact the bench height results.

At Your Spinning Wheel

HANDSPINNING DYNAMICS

Spinning is a smooth, controlled activity. A traditional spinning wheel is powered by a consistent treadling pace, which controls the speed at which the wheel rotates and drives the twist needed to create yarn from any fiber. While treadling, the spinner's fingers, hands, and arms keep up the pace, drafting the fiber and guiding the twist. If you're a spinner, you're well aware of just how important a chair is for your comfort. The chair you sit on at your wheel needs to fit your proportions and support your legs and back, while allowing your arms the freedom to draw out and/or back from the spindle or orifice without restriction. (See more on this topic in Chapter 4.)

You will need a helper to take accurate measurements (these cannot be taken without assistance). A yardstick or a rigid tape measure will yield the most accurate results.

OTHER CONSIDERATIONS

E-spinners, small electric devices that work very much like a spinning wheel only at a consistent speed for drafting and loading the bobbins and minus the treadles, are more popular today than ever. How does a person who uses an e-spinner measure themselves for a Spinner's Chair? In this case, the spindle (orifice) height is what really matters. For optimal comfort when spinning, we recommend that the e-spinner be used while placed on a low table, with a height of 24–26 inches. This arrangement mimics the orifice height of most spinning wheels. The spinner's leg length is measured as below.

Just as some weavers have more than one loom, spinners often have several wheels they put to use. Here, too, we recommend that spinners compute the chair height from the wheels they use the most, and then average that number.

DETERMINING YOUR BEST SPINNER'S CHAIR HEIGHT

Your Body Measurements

LOWER LEG LENGTH (LLL)

While standing barefoot or in the footwear you'd normally wear while spinning, measure from the floor up to the back of your knees, just where the crease would be were you to bend your knee. This measurement typically ranges from 16 to 19 inches. If one leg is shorter than the other, use the longer measurement.

ELBOW HEIGHT (EH)

Seated on a hard surface, relaxed but not slouching, bend your elbow to form a 90-degree angle, with your forearm horizontal and your upper arm vertical. Have your helper measure from the bottom of your elbow down to the top of seat. This number usually ranges from 8 to 12 inches. If your arms measure differently, go with the shorter measurement.

SEAT WIDTH

While seated as above, place a yardstick across your lap and measure from the outside of one thigh to the outside of the other. Or, if you prefer, you could take this same measurement by sitting on your yardstick.

SEAT DEPTH

Still seated, take the measurement from the back of your knee at the crease to the back of your buttocks on the seat.

BACK HEIGHT

Finally, measure from the top of the seat behind you to the top of your shoulders.

Your Wheel Measurements

Two measurements on your wheel(s) are all that are needed. First and foremost is the treadle height. Second and of less importance is the spindle height. Remember, the treadles redefine the height of the floor as compared to the body while spinning.

TREADLE HEIGHT

Spinning wheels have two types of treadles, determined by where the treadle pivots or rocks, as decided by the maker of the wheel. The pivot point will be either under the spinner's heel or just under their arch. The former generally measures 1½–1¾ inches from the floor to the top surface of the treadle at its pivot point,

At Your Kitchen Counter

BARSTOOLS

Historically, the bars in pubs and saloons are 42 inches high to allow the bartender an appropriately sized space for drink preparation. It's also more comfortable for the customer to stand or lean at with a foot up on the brass rail. Accompanying barstools are 30 inches high, or 12 inches less than the bar height. This 12-inch distance is the standard difference factored when seats are used while eating. (This also is something to consider when choosing table and chair sets for your kitchen and dining room.)

Barstools are used at breakfast counters for eating and/or entertaining. An industry-typical breakfast counter height is 36 inches, the same as standard kitchen countertops. Using the rule above, these stools would be 24 inches high (36 – 12 = 24). Some designers will raise the counter to 42 inches, so as to provide separation between the kitchen and entertaining area. In this case, the 30-inch barstool is the accompanying choice.

With more work being done from home and the likelihood that doing so is going to become our new normal, people are using their counters for their laptops in place of a desk, and are sitting at the counter for longer periods of time. Proper seating needs to consider the person, both their size and their needs. Applying the same principles used in sizing the Weaver's Bench, Spinner's Chair, and Knitter's/Musician's Rocker will result in a more supportive and ergonomic barstool in which the arms rest comfortably relative to the keyboard and the feet may utilize the footrest.

As always, you will need another person to take your measurements, along with a yardstick or a rigid tape measure.

though a few models measure more than 2 inches. The latter treadle type ranges from 2 to 3 inches to the top of the treadle at its pivot point.

SPINDLE/ORIFICE HEIGHT

While a spindle and an orifice are not the same and cannot be used on the wheel at the same time, their placement on the wheel is the same, so we use the terms interchangeably here.

Measure from the floor up to the center of the spindle on your wheel. This distance is dependent on a number of choices made by the wheel maker, as well as on the style of wheel.

For more comfortable spinning, the spinner's elbow should be level with or even slightly higher than the spindle or orifice, though this is not necessary to make usable yarns and is mostly a matter of preference. Some spinners prefer longer draws off the point of the spindle. In those cases, and in some others, the spinner's elbow will be above or even perpendicular to the orifice's level. True control over one's wheel is dependent on a comfortable seat.

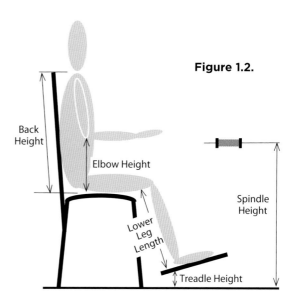

Figure 1.2.

Sample Calculation A

LLL = 18.5 inches
TH = 1.75 inches
Chair Seat Height (LLL + TH) = 20.5inches

Sample Calculation B

LLL = 17 inches
Treadle Height = 2.5 inches
Chair Seat Height (LLL + TH) = 19.5 inches

DETERMINING YOUR BEST BARSTOOL HEIGHT

Your Body Measurements

LOWER LEG LENGTH (LLL)

While standing barefoot or in your most commonly worn footwear, measure from the floor up to the crease at the back of your knees. Again, the range is typically 16–19 inches. If one leg is shorter than the other, use the longer measurement.

ELBOW HEIGHT (EH)

While sitting on a hard surface, relaxed but not slouching, hold your forearm horizontal with your upper arm vertical, making a 90-degree angle. Next, measure from the bottom of your elbow to the top of the seat. This typically ranges from 8 to 12 inches. If you have slightly different measurements on the right and left sides, use the shorter measurement.

SEAT WIDTH

While sitting as above, place a yardstick across your lap (or sit on it) and measure from the outside of one thigh to the outside of your other thigh.

SEAT DEPTH

Still seated, measure from the crease at the back of your knee to the back of your backside on the seat.

BACK HEIGHT

To make the stool more accommodating for those times when it's not being used as a work chair, its back needs to be shorter than that of the Spinner's Chair. The proper measurement here is from the top of the seat to the shoulder blades. This supports the lower back and still makes it easy to reach over the back of the seat as needed.

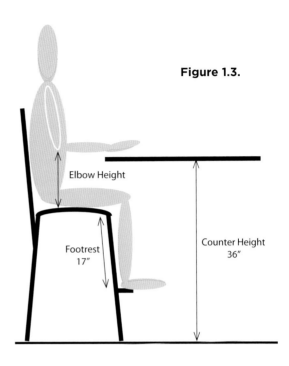

Figure 1.3.

Elbow Height

Footrest 17"

Counter Height 36"

FOOTREST

Like the seats, even the footrest has a lowered front stretcher. Its height measures approximately 17 inches below the front edge of the seat. If the user's lower leg length is less than 17 inches, the stretcher needs to be raised to 16 inches. If the LLL is longer than 18 inches, then the stretcher should be lowered to 18 inches.

Sample Calculation A

Counter Height (CH) = 36 inches
EH = 9 inches
Barstool Seat Height (CH - EH) = 27 inches

Sample Calculation B

Counter Height (CH) = 42 inches
EH = 8.5 inches
Barstool Seat Height (CH - EH) = 33.5 inches

BENCHES

The basic concept of benches and all my seats is a saddle shape, which allows a person to sit on the woven cord surface with minimal contact against the hard edges of the seat beneath their legs—that is, the person is suspended on a firm but flexible surface. The details of the frame construction are discussed in Chapter 5, and how the seat is woven is detailed in Chapter 6.

For now, let's just talk basics in terms of the history and development of my Weaver's Benches and how the comfort of my customers, combined with their user experience, has led to the benches' current iterations.

Weaving Benches

I make two primary styles of weaving benches: a classic, stationary type made to fit the weaver to their loom of 40-inch weaving width or less; and a bench that slides or rolls, allowing the weaver to seamlessly slide side to side across the width of a 40-inch or wider loom. Both styles can be made either backless or with a removable back, similar to the seat backs used on the Spinner's Chair. With or without this added back support, the bench on the sliding frame is built to be removed from its bottom frame in order to provide the weaver a more comfortable height from which to dress their loom. The latest design has the seat made to fit the weaver to more than one loom, since so many serious weavers possess multiple looms. The ability to break down this larger bench also helps it to be more portable for the on-the-go weaver.

STATIONARY BENCHES

In general, for looms with a breast beam height of 28–30 inches, a "standard" seat height is in the range of 20–22 inches.

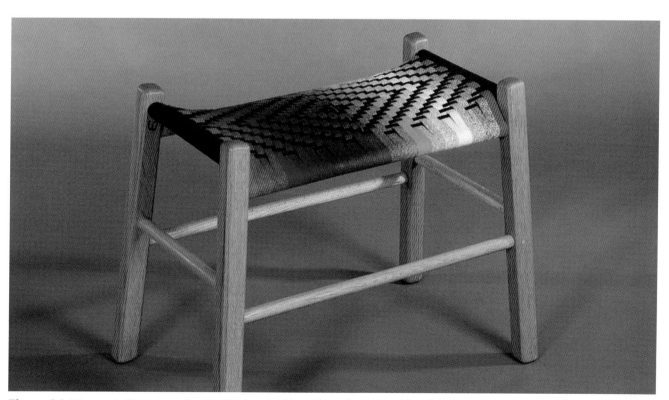

Figure 2.1. Weaver's Bench; red oak; diamond 2/2 twill; weft: Color Wheel, warp: Black. 21″ H x 13″ D x 25″ W. SPA

Figure 2.2. Weaver's Bench; ash; undulating 2/2 twill; weft: Purple/Grape, warp: Evergreen. 26″ H x 13″ D x 26″ W.

Figure 2.3. Weaver's Bench with back; maple; undulating 2/2 twill; weft: Arizona Cliffs gradient, warp: Light Brown/Cinnamon. Seat: 24.5″ H x 15″ D x 28″ W. Back: 18″ H. SPA

The bench in Figure 2.1 is one of a pair made in 2005. At Convergence 2004, tapestry weaver Tommie Scanlin requested a Weaver's Bench with the color wheel as the weft. Since she is a renowned tapestry weaver and teacher, I asked that she select the primary colors from the UKI color card. She was able to find the six primary and the six secondary colors she'd been envisioning. Using red, orange, yellow, green, blue, and purple, and making a 2-step gradient between each color wheel color, the eighteen shades were created. The second of these benches was made for Ellen. This began the process of my gradient cord blending. Details of various gradient techniques, as well as the yarns used, are covered in the appendixes.

When a seat height needs to be higher than 22 inches at a large multi-shaft, rug, draw, countermarch, or counterbalance loom, the front stretcher is lowered so that it may be used as a footrest (Figure 2.2).

To add extra support for production weavers or those with back problems, a seat back is added. Similar to the Spinner's Chair, the back is removable, and the seat is 15 inches deep.

SLIDING AND ROLLING SEAT BENCHES

Sliding Seat Bench

Inspired by the Fireside Commuter Bench by Gary Swett and the Kessenich Loom Bench by Bruce Niemi, the sliding seat bench has a removable seat, to be used for threading. To ease the movement, ultra-high-molecular-weight (UHMW) plastic is wrapped around the seat's side stretchers where they contact the rails.

Figure 2.4 shows the prototype sliding seat bench. The seat was made to be lifted off and used when dressing/threading the loom. The slide rails were 1½-inch diameter maple dowels. Flex of the dowels was a problem when the slider rails needed to be longer than 36 inches.

A few benches were made with a narrow stiffener attached to the bottom of the round rail dowel. Then, working with Hardwood Moulding here in Kingsport, Tennessee, a maple rail design was developed. The cross section was 2¼ inches high, 1¼ inches thick, and made in various lengths and cut to the measurements needed for the customer's bench. This greatly simplified making slider and rolling seat benches with rails as long as 60 inches.

Expanding the utility further, customers interested in the sliding Weaver's Benches also began requesting

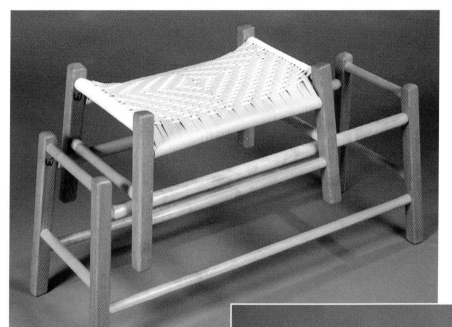

Figure 2.4. Sliding seat Weaver's Bench; white oak and maple; diamond 2/2 twill; weft: commercial tan, warp: commercial white. Seat: 18″ W x 13″ D x 12″ H. Total height: 21″ on 36″ rails. SPA

Figure 2.5. Sliding seat Weaver's Bench; maple; undulating 2/2 twill; weft: 5-color gradient in Kelly, Jade, Nassau, Special Purple, Purple; warp: Black. Seat: 24″ W x 13″ D x 14″ H. Total height: 27″ on 36″ rails. SPA

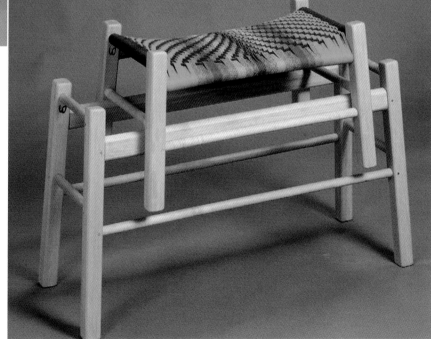

Figure 2.6. Sliding seat Weaver's Bench with removable back; cherry (maple slider rails); undulating 2/2 twill; weft: Nassau/Copen Blues, warp: Copen/Nassau Blues. Seat: 24″ W x 15″ D x 13″ H. Back: 18″ H. Total seat height: 25.5″ on 42″ rails. SPA

a removable-back option (Figure 2.6). Critical for this updated version is the addition of "keepers" in the front legs of the seat that fit under the slider rail to keep the weaver from flipping backward when leaning against the seat back (Figure 2.7). With the back added, the seat depth is 15 inches, providing greater stability and support of the weaver.

In 2014, Cathy Chung requested a loom bench to fit both her Baby Wolf and her Megado looms, which was achieved by fitting the bench to her Baby Wolf and then adding it to the sliding rails to make it perfectly compatible to her Megado (Figures 2.8 and 2.9). Since this worked so well and so many weavers have more than one loom, all subsequent sliding and rolling seat benches have been made with this configuration.

Figure 2.7. Sliding seat Weaver's Bench with back, detail of seat keeper.

Figures 2.8 and 2.9. Sliding seat Weaver's Bench; maple; advancing diamond 2/2 twill; weft: Flat Tencel Purple/Navy, warp: Flat Tencel Navy with Gold Fleck. Seat: 24″ W x 13″ D x 22″ H. Total height (on rails): 29.5″.

Rolling Seat Bench

Some weavers have knee and hip problems, making a sliding seat bench still too difficult to maneuver, so I experimented with rollers in place of the plastic strips. I found steel roller bearings a little noisy, so on later versions I replaced them with white Delrin plastic bearings (Figure 2.10).

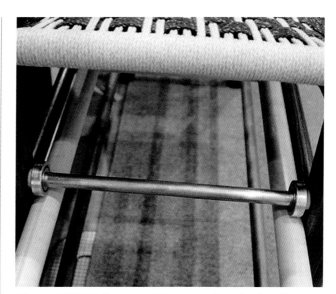

Figure 2.10. Rolling seat Weaver's Bench, detail of rollers.

3

STOOLS

The second iteration of the bench design came in 1994, when a friend asked me to build a stool fitted for use at their kitchen breakfast bar. (Hence, the business became "Benches and Stools." Once chairs for spinners were requested and I knew I'd found my niche as a maker, I began using the name "Benches, Stools & Chairs," the name I still use today and the title for this book.)

I used the same principles I'd learned from fitting a weaver's bench to a loom, and applied them to fitting people to sit at their countertops and bars. Instead of one person performing the craft of weaving, I would need to take into account that there would be multiple people of different sizes eating, drinking, and conversing at different times and using the same stools to do so. Other, longer-duration activities might include working, studying, gaming, reading, and general entertainment while using a laptop or tablet on the counter or bar surface. Two main considerations arose:

1. For general use, there were the usual ergonomic standards to direct the stool dimensions.
2. Individuals using their laptops for extended times would require considering their body dimensions relative to the counter and laptop keyboard, similar to how we measure a person to their loom or spinning wheel.

The usual ergonomic standard for a barstool seat height is to subtract 12 inches from the bar or counter height. Today's kitchen counters are typically 36 inches high, which would mean a stool height of 24 inches. Some homes have a breakfast bar, often used to separate the kitchen area from the eating nook or the family room. These surfaces are taller than the standard counter, at 42 inches high. Deducting 12 inches, the appropriate stool height here would be 30 inches. Interestingly, at a pub, bar, or cocktail lounge, where patrons tend to linger, the bar height is also typically 42 inches, with a stool height of 30 inches.

In consideration of sitting comfortably for extended time periods, I made the stool seats 15 inches deep and 20 inches wide. I also lowered the stretchers to 17 inches below the seat rails, making them suitable for use as footrests.

Figure 3.1. Barstool; maple; undulating 2/2 twill; weft: Oatmeal, warp: White. 20″ W x 15″ D x 24″ H, with stretchers as footrests.

Saddle Stool

Like many designs, the evolution of the trapezoidal Saddle Stool came from different inspirations. When I was a member of the Houston Woodworkers Club in 1995, the winter project challenge was to make a usable piece that used neither 90- nor 45-degree angles, which led to the Saddle Stool. All these years later, the original stool is still used as a work stool in my wood shop.

The Saddle Stool frame uses the 5-degree leg splay, only with an 18½-degree trapezoid for the seat and stretchers/footrests. The seat depth allows the user to sit "side saddle." The trapezoidal seat shape, besides being comfortable to sit on, also allows for easier placement at curved countertops.

The example in Figure 3.2 was made in 2006.

In 2014, a pair of Saddle Stools with removable backs was ordered for use as computer workstation seats at the homeowner's breakfast bar (Figure 3.3). The customer's elbow height was 10⅛ inches and the countertop height was 36 inches, so the seat heights were made at 25½ inches. (For a reminder on the specific calculations used to compute seat height, see Chapter 1.)

Figure 3.2. Saddle Stool; walnut; advancing 2/2 point twill; weft: Chocolate Chips, warp: Light Nugat. 20″ D x 7″ Front W/18″ Back W x 24″ H.

Figure 3.3. Saddle Stools with back; cherry; advancing 2/2 diamond twill seat; weft: Dark Lichen, warp: Light Lichen. 20″ D x 7″ Front W/20″ Back W x 25½″ H.

4

CHAIRS

During the development of the Weaver's Bench, some handspinners from the Contemporary Handweavers of Houston were asking for a bench that could be used at their wheels. Member Pat Wagner-Thompson asked whether hers could be made as a chair. I made Pat a fixed-back chair, fitted to her wheels. However, I discovered one design flaw when she and I met to hand off her new chair: We were barely able to get it inside her vehicle, a moderate-sized sedan. With some effort, we did eventually get that chair into the car that day, but the issue is what planted the seed in my mind for a more transportable chair for spinners.

Soon after, Ellen and I moved to Kingsport, Tennessee. I was still considering a career as a furniture maker, and so I began showing my work at both furniture shows and fiber shows. I had made a chair using butternut for the frame and soon learned that this type of wood was not suitable as chair wood, as the chair back broke a few inches above the seat. To save the seat, I made a separate back from extra butternut and fitted it to the seat with screwed-on "wings" affixed to the back of the legs.

At the next fiber show, spinners began placing orders, and my future would soon be sealed. In an effort to keep the chairs' breakdown as simple as possible, I replaced the machine screws (which would have meant the user having to carry a screwdriver along with any other spinning supplies) with simple knobs and brass-threaded rods. The chair backs were now easily removable, and the chair was far more mobile for bringing to meetings, festivals, classes, and the like.

Spinner's Chair

The basic design of this chair hasn't changed since 2000 (Figure 4.1). The seat frame is based on the Weaver's Bench with 5-degree compound leg angles. Since spinners sit at their wheels for extended times, the seat depth needed to be sufficient to fully support the individual from their back to a few inches short of the back of their knees. The back angle is about 5 degrees and tapers in at the top, following the angle of the back legs. This, and the

fact that there are no chair arms, keep the spinner's arms free to make long draws when desired, without needing to awkwardly swing the elbow over any obstacles.

After a few spinners had used their chairs for six to twelve months, they commented that the front stretcher was too low, preventing them from tucking their feet under the chair. The side and front stretchers were then

Figure 4.1. Spinner's Chair; maple; advancing 2/2 twill; weft: Oatmeal, warp: White. Seat: 22″ W x 19″ D x 19″ H. Back: 24″.

Figure 4.2. Spinner's Chair; cherry; advancing 2/2 twill; weft: Chocolate/Rust, warp: Rust/Chocolate. Seat: 22" W x 17" D x 17" H. Back: 24".

Figure 4.3. Knitter's Rocker; walnut; advancing 2/2 twill; weft: Chocolate Chips, warp: Light Nugat. Seat: 20" W x 18" D x 17" H. Back: 22". Skids: 34" L.

spaced 6 inches down from the seat rails. The back stretcher remained at 9 inches to support the back at 5 degrees (Figure 4.2).

Knitter's Rocker

My mother was a petite woman, only about 5 feet tall, and loved to knit, but because of her small stature, finding a comfortable knitting chair had been difficult for her. Eventually she found two folding, antique-replica, armless rockers, which she used for years. She liked that there were no arms to get in the way of her elbows, which made it easy to reach for yarn and needles in the baskets at her side. In honor of my mother, I came up with the Knitter's Rocker.

My first Knitter's Rocker order was for a fixed-back rocker based on the dining Side Chair (see Chapter 7).

Figure 4.4. Knitter's Rocker; cherry; advancing 2/2 twill; weft: Turk/Duck, warp: Natural. Seat: 22″ W x 16″ D x 15.5″ H. Back: 24″. Skids: 36″.

Figure 4.5. Musician's Rocker; maple; Black Watch Plaid, typically woven in 2/2 twill. Seat: 24″ W x 17.5″ H x 21″ D. Back: 29″. Skids: 40″.

The idea for putting rocker skids on a Spinner's Chair came from a customer who had purchased a sliding seat Weaver's Bench for her home in West Virginia. She liked to knit, and commuted weekends from her residence in Washington, DC, to the family's West Virginia home. Transporting a rocker with a removable back would be easy in her SUV and would mean having to only own the one chair.

MUSICIAN'S CHAIR AND ROCKER

Friends who are guitarists tend to like the comfort of the Spinner's Chair, the custom fit of its height and seat dimensions, and its narrow back, which allows for plenty of elbow room. More than one such friend has ordered a pair, requesting one chair (similar to a Spinner's Chair) for performances and a rocker (similar to a Knitter's Rocker) for practice.

5

FRAMES

I owe a debt of gratitude to the humble footstool/leg rest I inherited from my father, as it (and my desire to improve on its functionality) has served as the framework of my comfort seating concept. The seating discussed in Chapters 2, 3, 4, and 7 all evolved from this basic footstool/leg rest and my desire to create an inherently comfortable surface on which a person could rest their feet or legs while sitting in a chair.

Making a solid wood stool (see Photo 5 on page ix), even one with rounded edges, was out for these important reasons: Adding a pillow or upholstery would either cover up beautiful wood or add problems in sourcing appropriate fabric and padding; the edges of the stool could still cut into the back of the user's legs; and many common designs were too heavy and awkward to move, had edged legs that wouldn't slide on carpet or rugs, or were top heavy, causing the stool to tip over when trying to slide it away while getting up from the stool. I wanted something better, and through much trial and error, that's what I've created.

The basic concept of my seats is that the seat rails are separated and placed higher on the sides as compared to those on the front and back. This lets the woven seat, discussed in Chapter 6, naturally develop a saddle shape—mathematically called a hyperbolic paraboloid—just like a horse saddle. After a few experiments separating the rails from 1 inch to 4 inches, I decided that 2 inches worked well for a bench that is 13 inches deep and 24 inches wide (a good-sized starting point for a Weaver's Bench).

One of the problems with most weaving benches is that they are heavy and awkward to move when the weaver needs to get up or reposition themselves at the loom. A light, easy-to-move frame was needed, so I came up with a frame that has straight legs, with 1-inch-diameter dowels for the rails and stretchers. Spacing of 8–10 inches between the rails and corresponding stretchers works well, and for most applications I settled on 9-inch spacings. For stability, I tried splaying the legs from 4 to 7 degrees, at first just front to back. When I found 5 degrees to be most visually pleasing, this splay became a "standardized" compound 5 degrees (front to back and side to side), featured in all

my seat designs. For comfort, the tops of the legs were rounded. Rounding the bottoms similarly meant that the bench would slide smoothly on carpet.

All combined, a woven seat, a light frame, splayed legs, and rounding the bottoms of the legs meant that when a weaver was at their loom, they could slide the bench to a comfortable position and then move it with only a simple nudge of the leg when needing to stand. An unintentional side benefit of an open frame with a flexible, cord-woven seat is that the bench can flex up to ¾ inch to fit a non-flat floor. The seat's surface also helps absorb the weight of the user, leading to less stress on (and damage to) their joints.

Weaver's Bench Frame

JIGS

I began my full-time furniture endeavor with far fewer major woodworking tools than one might expect. As I was working out the basics of my bench design, I had only a 14-inch band saw, a Delta Unisaw table saw, a Craftsman drill press, and a small planer in my workshop. Adjusting the table angle on the drill press was awkward at best. As for the Unisaw, setting up for the compound angles on the leg bottoms was complex, and cutting them was nerve-racking in terms of safety. Setting up again after using the tools for other projects was time consuming and difficult, especially as I needed the angles to be repeatable. I needed to make jigs for accuracy and safety in machine work as my bench, stool, and chair making went full time. This was my process:

First, I dedicated a simple miter saw to making just the compound mitered cuts on the bottoms of the legs, setting the tilt to 5 degrees and bolting it to prevent any possibility of messing things up by using it for other projects. Since some simple 5-degree cuts are also used for chair backs, the miter angle was left adjustable and a setup block was made to reliably set the angle to 5 degrees.

Next was the jig for the drill press, used to drill the rail and stretcher mortises at 5 degrees (Figure 5.4). Using the dimensions of the drill press table and some trigonometry,

BASIC CALCULATIONS

Stretcher Length = Rail Length + (2 x (RS x sin 5°))
Sample calculations for Rail Length = 24 inches
  RS = 6 inches – Stretcher Length = 25 $\frac{1}{32}$ inches
  RS = 9 inches – Stretcher Length = 25 $\frac{9}{16}$ inches
  RS = 17 inches – Stretcher Length = 26 $\frac{31}{32}$ inches

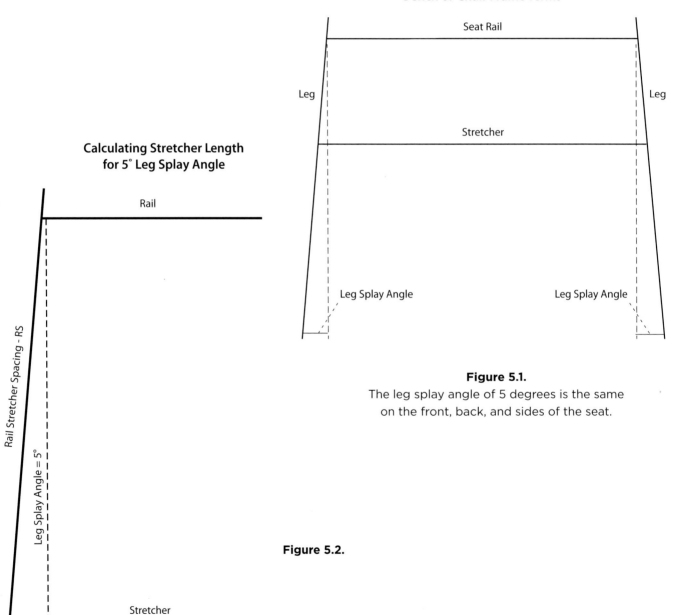

Bench or Chair Frame Terms

**Calculating Stretcher Length
for 5° Leg Splay Angle**

Figure 5.1.
The leg splay angle of 5 degrees is the same
on the front, back, and sides of the seat.

Figure 5.2.

I came up with a 5-degree tilted table, which was clamped in place on the drill press (Figure 5.5). I added a fence to keep the long leg stock stable during drilling, as well as a setup block made to align the table with the drill bit, centering the bit/mortises on the legs. Common mortise spacings (6 inches and 9 inches) were marked on the table, minimizing the need to lay out those mortises on each leg (Figure 5.6). This ensured leg pairs matched around a bench or chair.

Figure 5.3. Setup block for the 5-degree tilt and miter angles.

Figure 5.4. 5-degree mortise drilling table.

Figure 5.5. Detail, 5-degree mortise drilling table.

Figure 5.6. Spacing layout marks on the 5-degree mortise drilling table.

Chairs (and Saddle Stools) with trapezoidal seats necessitated the making of angled blocks to drill the compound angle mortises for their sides, at 5 degrees for the chairs and 18½ degrees for the Saddle Stools. My Arm Chair and the Fan-Back Rocker required special "tall" blocks to accommodate the angled legs and arm supports.

Figure 5.7. A 5-degree block for compound angle mortises.

Figure 5.8. An 18½-degree block for compound angle mortises on Saddle Stools.

LAYOUT TEMPLATES

To make the angled legs for fixed-back chairs and the leg/arm supports for the Fan-Back Rocker, precise templates were needed to cut matching pieces. Initially, I used ¼-inch masonite, but after a few chairs I saw that the template edges were wearing unevenly. To make stronger templates, I switched to ¼-inch translucent plexiglass. Three templates were made: 10 degrees, 15 degrees, and 20 degrees (Figure 5.9). Given the 5-degree leg splay, I used these to translate into respective back angles of 5 degrees, 10 degrees, and 15 degrees. The 20-degree template was also used for cutting the front arms of the Desk Chair. A 1¾-inch-wide template was made to facilitate layout of thickness for cutting on the band saw.

CUTTING, DRILLING, AND SHAPING

When I started out in Houston, Texas, I was able to easily get 8/4 rough-sawn lumber in most any wood species because Houston was an international port. With my small shop planer and professional table saw, the square 1¾-inch legs could be cut in a couple of hours. Using a No. 5 Stanley plane and a No. 151 and No. 53 Stanley spokeshave, the edge chamfers and rounding of the tops and bottoms of the legs added another couple of hours to the process.

After moving to Kingsport, Tennessee, imported exotics were less available. However, North American hardwoods of maple, walnut, cherry, red oak, and white oak were readily available locally because major furniture companies

Figure 5.9. Angles of 20 degrees, 15 degrees, and 10 degrees.

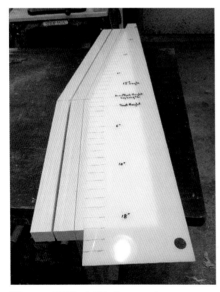

Figure 5.10. A 15-degree leg layout and cut.

Figure 5.11. Side Chair; maple; Fibonacci; weft: Red, warp: Wine; 5-degree legs with 10-degree back using the 15-degree layout template. Seat: 23″ W x 17″ H x 17″ D. Back height: 24″.

had shops and factories in the area. Also, many North American hardwoods are grown in the nearby Appalachian and Adirondack Mountains for commercial use. I continued with the same process for three to four years, using these hardwoods. Development of the Side Chair (Figure 5.11), Arm Chair, Settle, and Straight- and Fan-Back Rockers necessitated adding a better shop planer, an 18-inch band saw, a bigger dust collector, and a larger stationary belt sander to my shop setup.

As orders increased, producing all the leg stock from rough lumber for each Weaver's Bench and Spinner's Chair was time consuming, even though I found this work creatively satisfying. Benches and Spinner's Chairs use straight leg and back parts and, by happenstance, I learned of a shop in Kingsport called Hardwood Mouldings. Owner Chris Jones and his employees had the machinery to custom make and/or match any moldings a person could desire, and they had suppliers for the lumber. We worked out the basic linear stock I needed: 1¾-inch square with ¼-inch chamfers on all four edges. They could produce 8–14-foot lengths of the leg stock in the five hardwoods I needed, which I would then cut to length. I could estimate how much leg stock I would need for the next ten to fifteen orders and call the shop. Chris and his employees would then factor my order into their schedule.

WEAVER'S BENCH FRAME—CUT AND DRILLING

The bench being made in the following photo sequence is 22½ inches high by 24 inches wide and 13 inches deep.

For the 22½-inch seat height, the leg length needs to be 24½ inches long, and the rough-cut length needs to be 24¾ inches to accommodate the 5-degree compound cut for finished length.

Figure 5.12. Layout of rough leg length.

Figure 5.13. Marking rough leg length at 24¾ inches.

Figure 5.14. Setting length stop for cutting matching legs.

Figure 5.15. Leg length layout mark at the left side of the saw blade.

Figure 5.16. A "witness mark" is made on the leg before cutting, so the two legs can be matched later.

Figure 5.17. After rough cutting, the witness marks are used to pair the front and back legs. Single marks designate the bench sides, and double marks designate front and back. The marks are used to cut the legs to their final length with the compound 5-degree angles oriented correctly.

Figure 5.18. The witness marks are used for laying out mortises for the side rails and stretchers, as well as for the front and back rails and stretchers.

Figure 5.19. Mortise layout with leg centers marked.

Figure 5.20. Side rail mortise drilling using a 1-inch carbide Forstner bit. For speed and accuracy, the 5-degree jig is used on the drill press.

Figure 5.21. Front rail mortise drilling showing the 2-inch spacing relative to the side rail mortise.

Figure 5.22. The spokeshaves used for shaping the tops and bottoms of the seat legs: top, Lie-Nielsen Flat-Bottom Boggs; bottom, Stanley No. 151.

SHAPING

The WT monogram is branded on the right rear leg, below the side rail mortise.

Figure 5.23. WT brand and branding iron.

Before shaping the top and bottom of each leg, the sides are sanded using a belt sander with 120-grit sanding belt to remove minor surface imperfections and the smoke stains caused by the monogram branding.

The No. 151 is used to chamfer the edges and create the rough rounding of the corners of the legs. The Lie-Nielsen Boggs flat spokeshave is then used to smoothly round the edges and corners.

Figure 5.24. A leg clamped vertically in a bench vise.

Figure 5.25. Chamfered edges.

Figure 5.26. Rounded edges, beginning.

Figure 5.27. Corners rounded and all sanded with 120-grit belt paper.

Once all four legs are shaped, they and the stretchers are then sanded with 220-grit sanding paper. Everything is now ready for final glue-up.

GLUE-UP

I use and recommend Titebond II Extend for all joinery glue-ups. It is water resistant and has an 8–10-minute working time, which minimizes the need to rush assembly. The side leg pairs are glued first since they are smaller and easily adjusted to lie flat to check their match.

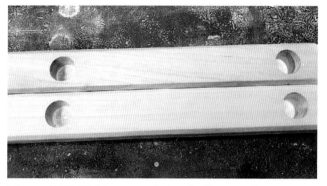

Figure 5.28. Thinly spread glue in the mortises.

Figure 5.29. Stretcher and rail are fully seated in the leg.

Figure 5.30. Leg flipped to seat the stretcher and rail into the opposite leg.

The process is repeated for the other side.

Figure 5.31. The side leg pairs are stacked to verify that the two sides match exactly and are not twisted.

Figure 5.32. Side view of the front and back rails and stretchers, now glued, and the bench being checked to sit flat.

Figure 5.33. Front view of the glue-up.

Figure 5.34. Tools for pegging the stretchers: ¼-inch bit with depth stop set at 1⁹⁄₁₆ inches, 1⁹⁄₁₆-inch maple or walnut pegs (tip tapered with pencil sharpener), lightweight carver's mallet, peg set dowel, Stanley No. 93 plane (set flush), Japanese flush-cut saw, 220-grit sandpaper.

STRETCHER MORTISE/TENON PEGGING

Gluing the rails and stretchers into the leg mortises with the Titebond II works well. However, over time and with regular use, the joints are flexed repeatedly, and any glued joint will ultimately loosen and pull apart. To prevent or minimize this type of failure, the stretchers are strengthened with ¼-inch maple or walnut cross pegs. (The seat rails are held together by the tightly woven seat.)

Each stretcher tenon is cross-drilled with 1⁹⁄₁₆-inch holes and a peg driven nearly flush. The peg is then trimmed flush with a Stanley No. 93 Rabbet Plane or cut flush with a flush-cut pull saw and subsequently sanded with 220-grit sandpaper.

Figure 5.36. Peg placed and then tapped until seated in the hole.

Figure 5.35. Peg hole, drilled.

Figure 5.37. Peg trimmed and sanded flush.

CORD ATTACHMENT

Traditional seat-weaving methods such as those discussed by Brandy Clements in the Foreword of this book use staples, brads, or nails to attach the weaving materials to the frame. Over time, these metal pieces create permanent holes that damage the wood and eventually can rust and break off. A Danish cord–style seat may have as many as 150-plus nails.

I wanted to make it easier for future craftsmen to reweave a bench or chair, so I developed my own wood-pegging technique (discussed in Chapter 6, along with the process of warping and weaving).

Figure 5.38. Side rail holes for pegging warp and spacing cords.

The holes for attaching the warp cord are horizontal in the side rails; the holes for attaching the spacing cord are at an angle.

Figure 5.39. The front and back rail holes for pegging weft cord.

Figure 5.40. Tall bench frame.

I use a natural Danish finishing oil as the final finish on 99 percent of my pieces. In addition, I recommend that my customers use a good, hard paste wax once a year. I like Lundmark Clear Paste Wax, which is 100 percent carnauba wax mixed with a softener that makes for easy, even application and then evaporates, leaving just the wax. Do note that care needs to be taken to buff the surfaces within 30 minutes of applying the wax.

Spinner's Chair Frame

Besides having a back, the main difference between a chair frame and a bench frame is that the chair seat is trapezoidal versus rectangular. This requires different calculations for the front and back rails. The stretchers, however, still follow the bench calculations relative to the seat rails. Figure 5.41 shows how the rails are calculated.

Once the chair seat frame is glued up, the back frame is then made to fit. Photos later in this section illustrate that process.

Calculating Chair Seat Rail Length

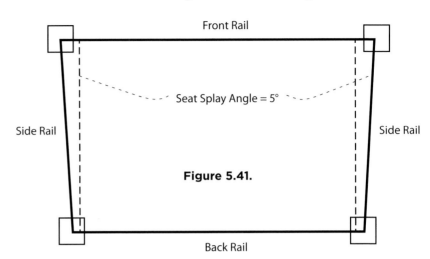

Front Rail

Seat Splay Angle = 5°

Side Rail   Side Rail

Figure 5.41.

Back Rail

SPINNER'S CHAIR FRAME ASSEMBLY

The legs and rails/stretchers here are cut the same way as described in the "Weaver's Bench Frame" section. Once the legs are rough cut to the appropriate length, they are witness marked to indicate the front, back, and sides.

Figure 5.42. Left and right sides are marked at an angle with the fronts noted.

The legs are then cut to their final length, just as they would be for a bench.

Figure 5.43. Compound 5-degree leg bottoms.

Since the seat is trapezoidal, the side mortises are drilled at compound 5-degree angles using the 5-degree angle block (Figure 5.44).

Figure 5.44. A 5-degree block for compound angle mortises.

The locations need to be marked and punched to ensure they are drilled into the centers of the legs. The rail stretcher spacings on the sides and front are 6 inches, and on the back they are 9 inches.

Figure 5.45. Legs arranged for marking side mortises.

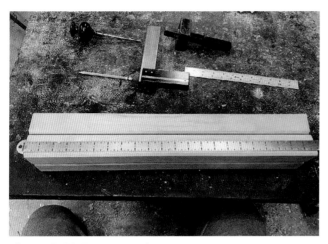

Figure 5.46. Layout tools.

Figure 5.47. Side mortises marked and centers punched.

Once all the mortises are drilled, the parts for the chair are shaped and sanded.

Figure 5.48. Chair seat frame parts finish-sanded with 220-grit paper.

Care needs to be taken during glue-up to maintain the leg orientations. The sides are glued first, just as they were in the bench glue-up.

Figure 5.49. Left side.

Figure 5.50. Glue spread thin in mortises.

Figure 5.51. Side assembled.

Figure 5.52. Side checked for flatness. Note the 9-inch spacing on the back leg and the 6-inch spacing on the front leg.

Figure 5.53. Checking that both sides match and are flat.

Figure 5.54. Final glue-up and checking that the frame sits flat.

After a 12–24-hour drying time, the stretchers are pegged, just as they were with the bench. Cord attachment holes are drilled similarly, though here the weft attachment holes are drilled only into the front stretcher. The reason for this approach is discussed in Chapter 6 in the "Chair Seat Weaving" section.

Figure 5.55. Finished seat frame. Note that the weft attachment holes are at the ends of the front seat rail.

CHAIR BACK

The Spinner's Chair and Knitter's Rocker backs are removable to allow for easier transport. The side benefit of the removable back is that weaving the seat and back separately is easier than trying to weave with the back in place.

The sides of the chair or rocker back are angled to match the leg splay of the seat frame. The purpose of this is to allow freedom of arm motion while the spinner is drawing out their fiber during the spinning process. Artistically, it enhances the trapezoidal flow to the chair.

There are four parts to the chair back—two sides and two rails. The back height is determined by measuring the customer's back height, from the seat up to the top of their shoulders. The sides are cut 10 inches longer, so that when the back is positioned on the back stretcher, it follows a 5-degree back angle, which comfortably supports the spinner or knitter.

Figure 5.56. Back uprights.

Rail mortises are cut at 5 degrees using a mortiser with an angle jig similar to the 5-degree jig used with the drill press. The "fish mouth" mortise/slot slides onto the back stretcher of the seat frame. The mortise/slot is a 26 mm hole then cut on the band saw. The 26 mm slot is 0.6 mm larger than the 1-inch (25.4 mm) stretchers. Shaping of the slot is similar to the shaping of the tops and bottoms of the legs.

Because the back is trapezoidal and each chair is custom fitted to the individual, variations arise in the length of the top and bottom back rails. Instead of calculating the lengths, it is easier to measure the spacings between the back sides.

Figure 5.57. Sides clamped on seat frame, aligned with the back legs and spacings measured.

For comfort, the back rails are curved slightly, which then curves the woven surface.

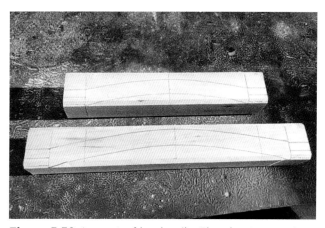

Figure 5.58. Layout of back rails. The shorter one is the top rail of the chair back.

Figure 5.59. Rough cutout of the back rails.

Figure 5.60. Dry fitting the back rail tenons into the upright mortises.

Figure 5.61. Dry fitting the back parts.

Figure 5.62. Rechecking the dry-fit back onto the seat frame to be sure all the angles are right and the tenons are tight in their mortises.

Figure 5.63. Finished chair back attached to the seat frame.

Figure 5.64. Back wings are created for each back leg, for firmly attaching the back to the seat. The steel screw, seen here, is just for positioning the wings during assembly. Threaded brass inserts (¼-20 threads) are used in the finished back uprights, placed 10 inches up from the seat stretcher.

To secure the back to the seat, ¼-20 threaded rods are glued into 1¼-inch-diameter by 1¾-inch-long wood blanks. The rods are left to protrude by 2 inches so as to run through the wings on the legs and fully into the threaded inserts.

Figure 5.65. Turning the back knobs.

After the glue has set, securing the ¼-20 threaded rods into the knob blanks, I use jam nuts to hold the knobs in the drill chuck. To shape the knobs, I use a combination of rasps, files, and sandpaper. I find this easier than using a lathe. I finish the wood with Danish oil.

Figure 5.66. Rasps and files for shaping the knobs, along with nuts for securing the knobs in the drill chuck.

Figure 5.67. Finished knobs.

Figure 5.68. Knob in wing on the chair leg.

Figure 5.69. Knob attached to back of chair.

Figure 5.70. Finished chair back on the seat frame.

ROCKER SKID GLUE-UP

All rocker skids for the Knitter's Rocker and the Fan-Back Rocker are cold-bent laminations. Seven 1¾-inch by ¼-inch by 46-inch pieces are used for each skid. The outside radius is 42 inches. To bend and hold the bent stack, the form needs to be strong enough to hold the seven clamps needed. As the lamina are clamped into the form, glue squeezes out, so ultra-high-molecular-weight plastic is used on the base and on the face of the form to keep the skid from sticking to the form. After 18–24 hours in the form, the skid is released.

Figure 5.71. Rocker skid bent lamination glue-up form, detail.

Figure 5.72. Rocker skid bent lamination glue-up form.

The cold-bent glue-up process needs to go smoothly and quickly. I use Titebond II Extend for two reasons: (1) the working time (before the glue sets up) is 8–10 minutes, so during the clamping into the jig the glue acts as a lubricant, letting the lamina slide easily; and (2) it is water resistant for times the rocker is used outside.

Seven ¼-inch lamina make a 1¾-inch-thick skid blank. That means there are six glued joints needing to be fully glued in succession. Then the stack is moved to the jig and sequentially clamped from the center out to the ends.

Figure 5.74. Applying glue uniformly across and along the lamina.

Figure 5.73. Rocker skid lamina: seven per skid, ¼″ thick x 1¾″ wide x 46″ long.

Figure 5.75. Seven lamina glued and stacked, ready to put in jig.

Figure 5.76. Lamina ready for clamping.

Figure 5.78. Clamping step 2, progressively bending the skid.

Figure 5.77. Clamping step 1, drawing the center into the jig.

Figure 5.79. Clamping step 3, clamps at each end of the skid keep the lamina flat on the jig.

Figure 5.80. Clamping step 4, done. Let it set for 12–24 hours.

Figure 5.81. Lamina, skid blank, and skid ready to attach to seat frame.

ROCKER SKID SHAPING LAYOUT

Once the skids are glued up, the pair need to be cut to length (proportional to the size of the rocker), the tails shaped, and the front also shaped to match. Correspondingly, the chair right and left skids need to fit under the chair legs at the matching angles and at the same places on the skids. If they don't match, the rocker will "crab" (move to one side) as it rocks.

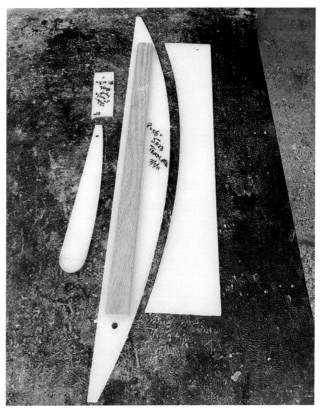

Figure 5.82. Skid nose and taper templates.

6

WEAVING

The basic development principle of my bench design has always been about creating a seat surface that is inherently comfortable, needing no additional padding. This quest led to a compound curved surface, an approximation of a hyperbolic parabola, or saddle shape. After experimentation with various traditional seat-weaving materials (see Foreword for more information) and rug- and tapestry-weaving methods and materials, I eventually settled on using ⅛-inch braided 100 percent cotton cord, as I found this cord to work best and to wear well. It is strong, flexible, and breathable, and it can even be treated with basic household water-repellent spray to resist stains. Please see the appendixes at the end of this book for more detailed information about the brand, colors, and color-blending methods I use when weaving my more colorful benches, stools, and chairs. (There is also a photo gallery for design inspiration.) I braid the yarns I use in my shop, using a commercial braider, into the ⅛-inch round cord I then weave with. The same ⅛-inch cord is commercially available in white and off-white, which is what I recommend to anyone starting out with my methods.

Commercial and consumer cotton cord is made with cotton or polyester as a core fiber. The polyester core cord is *not* recommended for seat weaving, as the cotton braid slides off the core during the weaving process.

Figure 6.1. Weaver's Bench and Spinner's Chair in advancing twill. SPA

41

This chapter will explain the weaving process for a Weaver's Bench. This process can be extended to other rectangular seats, such as dressing benches, barstools, footstools, and so forth. This bench process is then expanded to the trapezoidal seats and backs on the Spinner's Chairs, plus any other seating.

With a thick ⅛-inch cord, trying to weave the Shaker chair, as shown in the Foreword (Photo 4 on page vii), was impossible. In loom weaving terms, the warp threads (technically, these are wider cords here) need to be spaced enough to allow room for the weft to go under and over the warp cords during the weaving process. Even a spacing of two warp ends didn't leave enough space to weave a solid-looking surface.

After a few tests I discovered that twills, or weaving patterns that progress diagonally, provided solutions to multiple issues: a flexible seat, relative ease of weaving, and a wide variety of pattern options. Twills have great durability, too. In fact, denim jeans are a machine-woven twill fabric, chosen for durability and flexibility.

Custom sizing and fitting seats to individuals required using nonstandard dimensions, as discussed earlier in the book. A bench could vary from 20 to 28 inches wide and from 10 to 18 inches deep. Using simple weaving patterns such as chevrons or diamonds created problems in trying to center them. After multiple benches, I became bored.

I saw that seats with significant curvature don't actually allow for straight lines in the fabric. It depended on your perspective: What appeared to be a straight line from an overhead vantage point was a curve from a low angle at the front.

So why limit the patterns? Except for some larger furniture pieces, my bread and butter is variations of 2/2 twill. Simply changing the number of picks per shed causes the angle of the pattern to change, too. In weaving, 2/2 twills (an even weave of 2 warp threads and 2 weft threads) repeat every fourth shed, so progressively changing the picks per shed every 4 sheds creates apparent curves in the pattern. This is called an advancing twill (Figure 6.1).

Weaver's Bench

When I was first developing my woven design, I would sit on any old chair or bench while I wove the seats. When weaving shorter stools, I would sit on the floor. After sitting on the floor for about four hours, I would struggle to get up and my body was very stiff. I learned that I needed to heed my own advice, so I set out to build and weave a bench of my own to use specifically while weaving other people's custom seats.

The first bench was a frame measuring 21 inches high by 24 inches wide by 9 inches deep. I made the mistake of

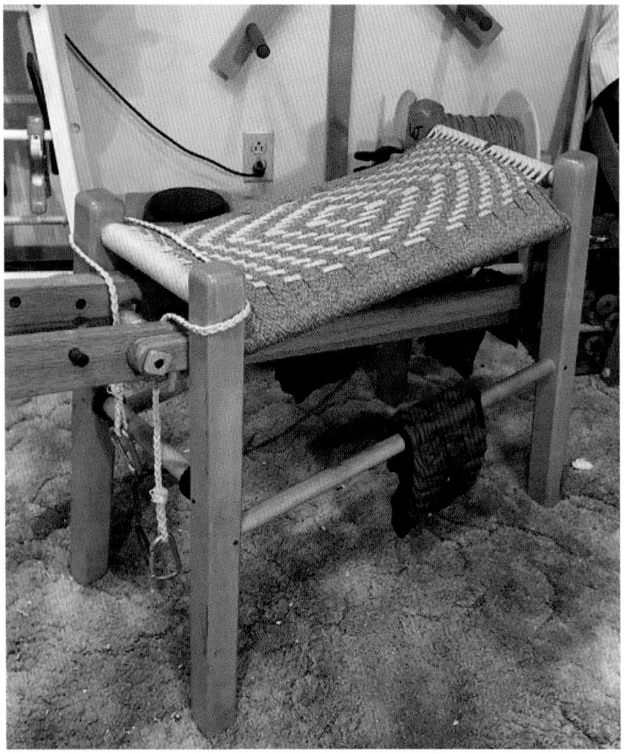

Figure 6.2. Saddle-style frame in maple; 10-pound ankle weight hangs on the stretcher; work rails are folded for storage. 21″ H x 24″ L; front: 9″ W; back: 11″ W.

Figure 6.3. Saddle-style frame in maple; secondary support stretcher, used for holding work rails, is at working height. 21″ H x 24″ L; front: 9″ W; back: 11″ W.

Figure 6.4. Work rails, unfolded, to support the frame being woven. Rails 29″ L to support a 28″ W frame.

Figure 6.5. Frame is positioned and weighted for weaving.

trying to stain the maple wood to look like cherry. (Lesson learned: Just use the desired wood to begin with.) Using a few clamps, I positioned a pair of 54-inch support rails to hold a bench frame at an angle while I sat straddled on the makeshift bench. Through trial and error, my current bench was made. It is essentially a saddle style, with the front and back rails higher than the side rails. (This is what allows me to sit with my legs straddled.)

A frame being warped is weighted down with a pair of 10-pound ankle weights to tension the warp uniformly. Once the warp is completed, the frame is positioned on the angled rails for weaving. The height of the work rails positions the frame at my elbow height, which allows me to comfortably weave. The angle of the rails sets the frame, so I'm comfortable weaving a 28-inch-wide frame.

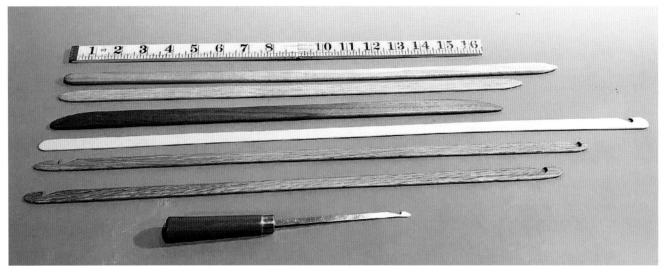

Figure 6.6. Examples of weaving tools: Top to bottom—shed sticks, 16″ to longer than 36″; hook sticks, 16″ to longer than 36″; short heddle hook, 6″ plus handle.

WEAVING TERMS

Fabric weaving terms will be used throughout this chapter and are defined as follows:

Warp: Cord wrapped side-to-side around the seat's side rails.

Weft: Cord woven front-to-back through the warp.

Shed: The separation of warp ends, through which the weft cord is woven.

Pick: One weft cord woven through a full (one row) shed.

WEAVING TOOLS

To keep the warp tension across a seat or back, the shed needs to open slightly more than the ⅛ inch of the (weft) cord. I make my shed sticks—used to hold open and then release the shed—from scrap cutoffs of maple, cherry, walnut, and oak. The various lengths are for seats ranging from 10 inches deep to back heights of 36 inches, and typical thicknesses are from ³⁄₁₆ to ¼ inch. The shed sticks' widths are usually from ½ to ¾ inch. To easily weave the stick through the warp pattern, the ends of the shed sticks are tapered, but not into sharp points. All the edges are rounded and sanded with 220-grit sandpaper and finished with a coat of natural Danish oil. With use, the cord will polish the wood even more.

To pull the weft through the shed for positioning, I use double-ended hook sticks. I use a single-ended hook stick for weaving the front of the chair backs. Both are similar to shed sticks, just slightly thinner and narrower so as not to drag while being pulled through the warp cord, and with ¼-inch hooks on each end (or on one end, for single-ended sticks). The ends are rounded so that the wood doesn't catch on the warp when being drawn through

Figure 6.7. Weaver's Bench; maple; 2/2 advancing diamond twill; weft: Champagne/Cinnamon, warp: Chocolate/Rust. 24″ W x 13″ D x 22.5″ H. SPA

to hook the weft. The double-ended hook sticks make alternating between weaving the top surface and drawing the weft over the bottom warp layer easier. Finishing is the same as for the plain shed sticks, and natural polishing comes with use.

If wood scraps are not readily available for making into shed sticks, narrow Navajo rug-weaving swords (known as battens) work well too.

As for pegging the warp and weft cords to the rails, I find a short heddle hook is best for pulling the cord through these holes. A heddle hook is also the most convenient tool I've found for weaving those last, very tight, 2–3 inches of a bench seat when a shed stick cannot be used. It is the only tool I've found capable of weaving the triangle sides of chair seats and backs.

The top surface of a bench is woven while the lower surface is not. Since the top surface of the seat is curved, the

Figure 6.8. Seat bottom showing the weft cords over the lower warp cords.

lower surface also needs to be curved. Therefore, the weft cord is pulled over the bottom warp surface and tensioned the same way as the top surface, effectively pulling it into a corresponding shape. Since the warp is continuously wrapped around the seat rails, the tension of the top and bottom helps create the firm seat.

BENCH SEAT WEAVING

The basic steps for weaving a curved bench seat are:
1. Select a pattern to weave.
2. Calculate the amount of warp needed for the seat.
3. Measure the warp.
4. Wrap the warp around the side rails of the bench.
5. Tension the warp on the frame.
6. Space the warp on the rails.
7. Weave the seat with tension to develop the saddle-shape seat.

I recommend that you always measure about 1 yard more than the calculated total, to give yourself working length at the end of wrapping on the warp. I made myself a warp winder that is 2 yards in circumference. (I'm fortunate that my arm span also happens to be 2 yards, providing another means of measuring.)

Once the warp is measured, it needs to be wound into a center-pull ball for wrapping onto the chair seat frame.

TOTAL WARP LENGTH

1. Measure the side rail length between the legs, RS.
2. Calculate the total number of warp ends, E.
   E = ((RS x 8) / 2) +2 (if you end up with an odd number, add 1 to make the number even)
3. Measure the distance between the two centers of the side rails, WS.
4. Calculate the length of one warp end, W.
   W = (WS x 2) + 3.2 (circumference of a 1-inch dowel)
5. Calculate the total warp needed (yards), WT.
   WT = (W x E) / 36

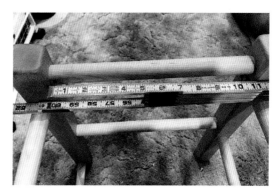

Figure 6.9. Side rail length (RS).

E = ((11 x 8) / 2) +2 = 46

Figure 6.10. Warp end length (WS).

W = (23.5 x 2) + 3.2 = 50.2 inches
WT = (50.2 x 46) / 36 = 64 yards

Figure 6.11. Two-yard warp winder.

Figure 6.12. Center-pull ball.

WARPING THE SEAT FRAME

Traditional seat weaving methods (as discussed in the Foreword) use tacks, nails, brads, or staples to attach the seat material to the frames. As a woodworker, I noticed that over time the metal would rust, making removal difficult. If the seat is rewoven multiple times over its life span, the subsequent restoration will require replacing the rails. Thinking ahead to future restorers, using wood pegs and wedging the seat cord into holes in the rails allows for easy removal, without wood damage and while still reusing the existing holes. With ⅛-inch cord, ¼-inch holes are drilled for easy cord insertion, and then ¼-inch poplar dowel pegs (⅞ inch long) are tapped in, wedging the cord tight. Poplar is soft and easily trimmed into wedges, and when driven into the hole, the peg and cord will compress tightly, with no glue needed.

Figure 6.13. Poplar wood pegs for attaching warp and weft to the seat rails of the bench.

Two holes are drilled in each side rail of the bench, one for attaching the warp (closest to the leg) and one for attaching the spacing cords (drilled at an angle).

Taking the warp end that is coming out of the center of the warp ball, use a weaver's short heddle hook to pull the warp end through the hole from the inside out, leaving a short portion of the warp exposed outside the hole (Figure 6.14). Drive the peg in flush to the rail, and then trim the cord flush (Figure 6.15).

Use the same procedure for attaching both warp and weft cord to the frame.

Figure 6.14. Heddle hook pulling cord through the hole in the rail.

Figure 6.15. Peg is driven flush next to the warp end, and then the cord is trimmed flush.

WRAPPING THE WARP

Wrapping is done in groups of ten. This lets you check for wrapping mistakes and helps ensure that your warp cords aren't crossed anywhere. The bench is weighted with 16–20 pounds. I prefer to use two 10-pound ankle weights, and in my workshops the students use two 1-gallon jugs of water. The weights are hung on the side stretchers for balance.

With the warp ball in your left hand, pull the warp under the seat rail, over the top and across the seat to the right-side rail; pull over and then under the right rail; and then pull the ball across to the bottom of the left rail and over the top. *Note:* When drawing from the left, the warp is on top; when pulling from the right, the warp is on the bottom.

After ten wraps are made, lay down the ball while you tighten the warp ends. Here's how to tension them: With your right hand holding the first warp end, pull vertically until the bench just lifts. With your left hand, grab the second warp end and lift, pulling any slack in the right hand and transferring it over to your left hand, and again lift the bench slightly. Holding the tension, grab the second warp end with your right hand, and with your left, grab the third end and pull up until the bench just lifts; repeat the process until the ten ends are taut. Wrap the slack under the right rail and, holding the tension, slide the group of ten together and clamp the tensioned warp end to the right side rail (Figure 6.16).

Repeat the process in groups of ten. There may be a small group (fewer than ten) at the end of wrapping. The last wrap is pulled under the right side rail and clamped to the back rail.

Figure 6.16. Ten tensioned warp ends clamped to the right side rail.

Check that the tension is equal on all ends. Draw your fingers across the warp, checking that each end flexes equally. If some feel looser, start with the first warp and repeat, pulling upward as in first tensioning and transitioning the slack to each end until it's equal across the bench. Clamp to the back rail (Figure 6.17).

Figure 6.17. Forty-six tensioned warp ends clamped to the back rail.

Without unclamping, pull the last warp end through the hole in the right rail, next to the back leg. Use your thumb to hold the last warp end to the top of the rail, and then unclamp and fully pull the warp through the hole. Pull tight under the rail and clamp to the back rail (Figure 6.18). Peg the warp into the hole, unclamp, and trim flush.

Figure 6.18. Warp is pulled through the hole and pegged, as was done at the start on the opposite side.

Figure 6.19. Warp trimmed flush.

With the warp fully tensioned and pegged, spread the warp ends, in pairs, across the side rails. This makes for ¼-inch spacing between the pairs (Figure 6.20).

Figure 6.20. Forty-six warp ends spread evenly in twenty-three pairs.

There are twenty-two spacings between the pairs. To keep the spacings from moving, two spacing cords are tightly wrapped between each pair around the rail, making for forty-four total ends per side. The circumference of a 1-inch dowel is approximately 3.2 inches, so 44 times 3.2 equals 141 inches, or 4 yards for each side, totaling 8 yards. Add another yard for crossing from right to left and for working length, meaning that you would measure 9 yards of warp cord. Peg and trim an end into the hole between the last warp pair. Tightly wrap the two cord ends clockwise around the rail between the warp pairs, filling the twenty-two spaces. When the last pair is reached, pull the cord across the lower side of the bench and over to the opposite side. Repeat the process, filling the spacings. Pull the cord through the hole between the warp pair. Peg and trim.

BENCH WEAVING

The pattern woven here is the 2/2 advancing diamond twill shown in Figure 6.7 (page 44). The weaving drawdown in Figure 6.23 provides the details of the weaving pattern.

Figure 6.21. Spacing cords between warp pairs (note how they are wrapped around the rail).

Figure 6.22. Tensioned and spaced warp.

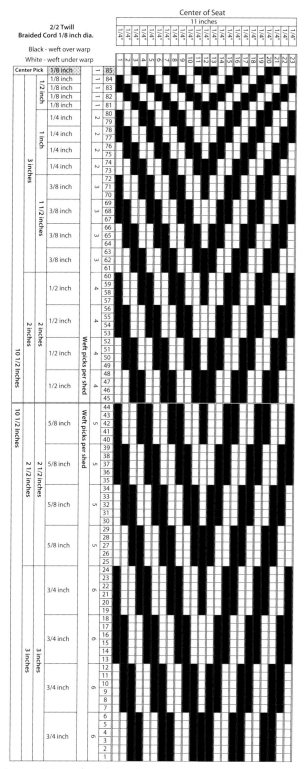

Figure 6.23. 2/2 advancing diamond twill drawdown.

Figure 6.24. Midpoints of the front and back rails are marked. The weaving pattern is marked on the front rail.

Figure 6.25. Close-up of weaving pattern marked on the front rail.

As shown in the drawdown, 4 sheds of 6 picks per shed is 3 inches; 4 sheds of 5 picks per shed is 2.5 inches; 4 sheds of 4 picks per shed is 2 inches; and 4 sheds of 3, 2, and 1 picks per shed adds up to 3 inches. How firmly the weft picks are packed impacts whether the weaving will progress at its written measurements. Adjustments may need to be made at the written marks as the weaving progresses, which is why it is so important to check.

Shed sticks and hook sticks are different lengths for use with different seat depths. A shed or hook of 18–20 inches works well for 13–15-inch seat depths. As mentioned earlier in this chapter, I make mine from scraps in the wood shop. Heddle hooks are used by weavers to thread warp yarn through heddles on their looms, and these are also useful in our seat weaving. I found a short (about 6 inches long) heddle hook among Ellen's weaving tools. The cord cutters I initially used were letter openers that had been given out at conferences I'd attended in my geophysics career. Later, safety box openers were developed. These work much better than the letter openers and can be found in the utility knife tool sections of any hardware store.

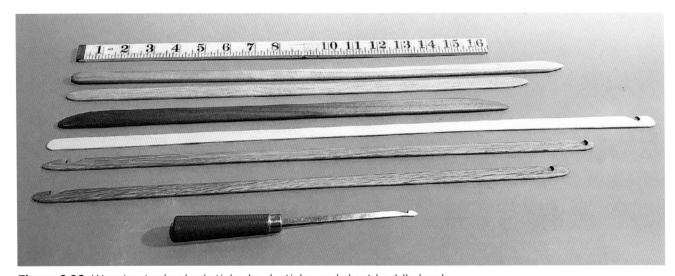

Figure 6.26. Weaving tools: shed sticks, hook sticks, and short heddle hook.

A shed of about ³⁄₁₆–¼ inch is all that is needed for weaving the weft. Any larger and it would unbalance the tension across the bench, uncentering the saddle shape. Any less of a shed height would create drag as the weft is pulled through it and across the warp cords.

Over time, I settled on weaving with weft skeins of about 12–15 yards each. I am not stopping too often to add a skein or spending too much time pulling the weft through the shed.

The weft cord is attached as shown in Figure 6.27.

Figure 6.27. Attaching weft to the front rail to begin weaving.

Once pegged to the front rail, the weft is wrapped around it once. This covers the peg, compensates for the 5-degree leg angle, and aligns the weft to work straight across the warp.

Using the hook stick, a weft loop is pulled/woven through the warp shed to the back rail. The weft is pulled tight, wrapped around the back similarly to the start on the front rail, and clamped to hold the tension.

Figure 6.28. Wrapping the first pick around the back rail.

The rest of the skein is pulled across, the tail end drawn under the back rail, over and across the lower warp with the hook stick, and under the front rail. This lower pass is then pulled tight and clamped to the front rail, starting the next weaving pass.

Figure 6.29. The shed stick was woven through the warp, opening the shed, and then the 6 picks were woven in the first shed.

An advancing diamond 2/2 twill is being woven. The center warp is marked with a contrasting cord. (I refer to this as the "Sheila Trick," as one of my first students had a difficult time seeing the middle warp end.)

You can see the centered 2/2 pattern in the shed: over 2, under 2, over 2, under 2, over 2, under 3 (the center of the diamond), over 2, under 2, over 2, under 2, over 2 (symmetric around the center warp end).

The twill pattern is seen in Figure 6.30.

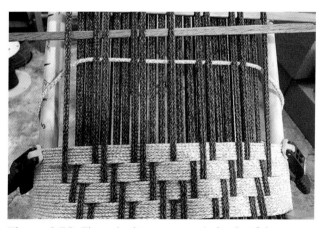

Figure 6.30. Three inches woven, 4 sheds of 6 picks each.

The second shed has the weaving shifted outward from the center with the sequence being over 1, under 2, over 2, under 2, over 2, under 2, over 1 (the center), under 2, over 2, under 2, over 2, under 2, over 1. Again, the shed is symmetric around the center warp end.

The progression continues in the third shed: under 2, over 2, under 2, over 2, under 2, over 3 (the center), under 2, over 2, under 2, over 2, under 2.

The fourth shed completes the 6-pick sequence and ends at the mark between the 6-pick and 5-pick sections of the pattern on the front rail.

Figure 6.31. Beginning the 5 picks per shed section. Note that the weaving pattern of the first 5-pick shed is the same as the first 6-pick shed.

A new skein is tied to the first skein. Note in Figure 6.31 that the end of the weft skein has been wrapped around the back rail and pulled up to lie on the top of the seat. A fisherman's knot is used to tie one skein to the next (Figure 6.32). The knot is made and tightened so that it can be hidden approximately in the middle of the seat (Figure 6.33).

Figure 6.32. The fisherman's knot is used to tie on a new skein. For long-lasting and best results, do not substitute another knot.

Figure 6.33. Tightened fisherman's knot.

Figure 6.34. Knot tightened and hidden between the upper and lower warp layers.

Figure 6.35. Five-pick section completed and 4-pick section begun.

Figure 6.36. Woven to the halfway point.

At the halfway point, the weaving pattern sequence reverses. Weaving the first half, a habit or rhythm develops, and the weaver needs to consciously think about what now needs to be done when inserting the shed stick in order to reverse the pattern. What has been woven is the same sequence to be woven, only in reverse order, matching the single-pick sheds, 2-pick sheds, 3-pick sheds, and so on. Take the time to count the picks per shed.

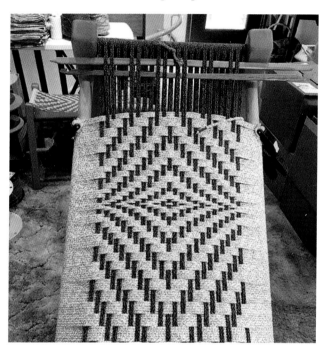

Figure 6.37. The three-quarters-completed point. Note the symmetry of the center diamond and the rest of the seat.

While weaving the last 2–3 inches, or 12–18 picks, the shed is very difficult to open with the shed stick, as is trying to pull the weft across with the hook stick. Also, reaching across the width of the bench is a stretch, so I turn the bench around on the workstand (Figure 6.39).

Figure 6.38. The 6-pick section begun, with 2½ sheds to complete.

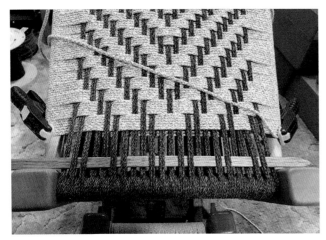

Figure 6.39. The bench reversed on the workstand. A thinner, more flexible shed stick is used as a guide for hand-picking the weft using the short heddle hook.

Figure 6.40. Even the thin, flexible shed stick cannot be used for the last shed.

Figure 6.41. Using a short heddle hook to weave the last shed.

Figure 6.42. Detail of weaving with a short heddle hook.

The last pick mirrors the first pick, with spacing wraps around the front and back rails. See Figures 6.27 and 6.28 (page 51).

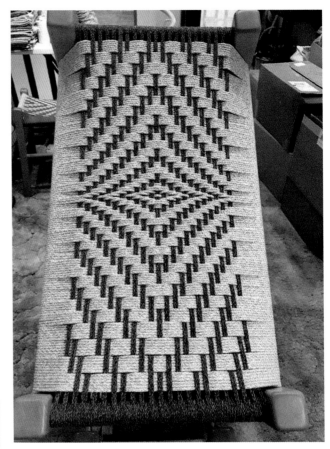

Figure 6.43. The finished seat.

Spinner's Chair

Weaving the seat and back of a Spinner's Chair uses the same tools and techniques as the Weaver's Bench. The center sections of the seat and back are actually rectangles, like a bench. The differences are the triangular side sections. The back side of the chair back needs to be woven as it's also used to hide the knots when adding weft skeins.

The weaving pattern for this chair is the 2/2 advancing twill.

This drawdown gives all the parameters needed to weave the seat and back of a chair. One of the advantages I have found with advancing twills is their ability to scale to different dimensions. Most important is measuring for the center of the front and back of the seat (and seat back) and then measuring the pattern from the center.

Figure 6.45. Seat frame with front and back center marks and advancing twill layout on front rail.

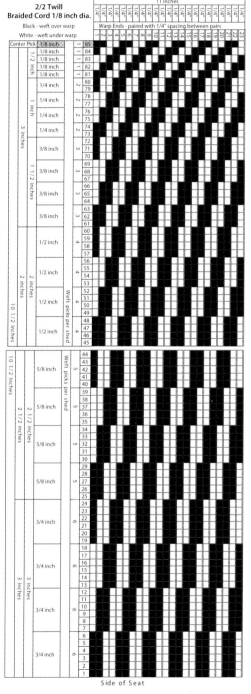

Figure 6.44. 2/2 advancing twill drawdown for a 24″ x 13″ bench.

Figure 6.46. Advancing twill layout detail.

CHAIR WARP MEASURING AND WRAPPING ON

To calculate the total length of the seat warp (which is similar to the bench calculation), measure at the front from the top center of the side rails (20½ inches) and at the back top center of the side rails (16½ inches). There are two ways to calculate the average single warp length:

1. (2 x 20.5 inches) + 3.2 inches = 44.2 inches
   (2 x 16.5 inches) + 3.2 inches = 36.2 inches
   (44.2 inches + 36.2 inches) / 2 = 40.2 inches

   or

2. (20.5 inches + 16.5 inches) + 3.2 inches = 40.2 inches
   The side rail length between the legs is 16 inches (16 inches x 4) + 2 = 66 warp ends
   Total warp length is (66 x 40.2 inches) / 36 inches = 73.7 yards

Figure 6.47. Seat warping.

Measure off 75 yards, accounting for working cord at the end. Wind a center-pull ball like the one in the "Bench Seat Weaving" section. Peg to the side rail, and wrap and tension the warp as you would for a bench. Then spread and wrap the spacing cords.

Figure 6.48. Seat warp spaced for spacing cords.

CHAIR SEAT WEAVING

The center section of the seat is the width of the back rail and is woven as a bench. Weaving the two side triangles is slightly different. Note in Figure 6.43 (page 54) that the pattern is measured from the center: 1-pick sheds = ½ inch, 2-pick sheds = 1 inch, 3-pick sheds = 1 ½ inches, 4-pick sheds = 2 inches, and 5-pick sheds = 2 ½ inches. I then wrote "16," which is the number of picks needed to fill the remaining 2 inches.

Weaving of the triangle is only on the top surface of the seat. Eight pairs of weft are needed, with each pair woven up and back to different warp ends. To lay out the warp ends to make these "turns," calculate the number of warp ends between turns.

33 ends / 8 turns = 4 warp ends between turns

In Figure 6.49, markers are tied to the appropriate warp ends. The red cord marks the line between the back rail and the corresponding location on the front rail, which is the base of the triangle. The shed stick and red alignment cord are in the first shed of the 5-pick shed section.

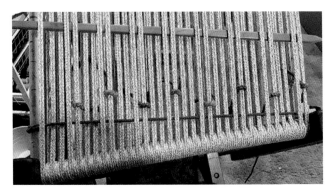

Figure 6.49. Triangle weaving layout.

To follow the advancing twill pattern, the triangle needs to be woven with 6 picks per shed. This means 2 sheds plus 4 picks to equal the 16 picks needed. Weaving starts at the leg, with the weft pegged as for a bench.

Figure 6.50. Peg at the start of the triangle weaving.

Figure 6.51. Woven triangle.

Using the heddle hook, weave the first weft pick up to the first marker, and then loop back to the front rail. Wrap once around the rail, and then weave the third pick in the same shed, up to the second marker; loop back to the rail. The fifth pick is woven in the next shed of the pattern, up to the third marker and back. The seventh pick is woven in the same shed, up and back to the fourth marker, and the ninth pick is woven up and back to the fifth marker. The eleventh pick is woven in the next pattern shed, up and back to the sixth marker. The thirteenth pick is woven in the same shed, up and back to the seventh marker, and the fifteenth pick is woven up and back to the eighth marker. The eighth marker is on the last/back warp end, and the sixteenth pick runs along the red alignment cord to the front rail.

Figure 6.52. Triangle woven and the 4 sheds of 5 picks.

Figure 6.53. Detail of the triangle and the 4 sheds of 5 picks.

Figure 6.54. Seat woven halfway.

Figure 6.55. Seat woven to the beginning of the 5-pick shed sequence.

Figure 6.56. Detail of the last shed where a shed stick can still be used.

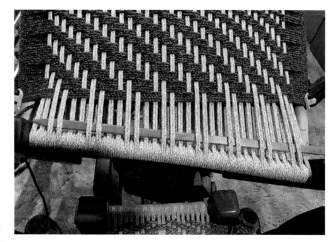

Figure 6.57. Seat reversed to more easily weave the right side.

The last of the 5-pick sheds and the triangle are woven using the heddle hook. The triangle weaving is the reverse of the left side, using the right-side triangle as the guide.

Figure 6.58. Detail of completed seat.

Figure 6.59. The last pick is pulled through the hole between the last two pick wraps on the rail and pegged.

Figure 6.60. Completed seat.

CHAIR BACK WEAVING

Spinner's Chairs have removable backs, and since the back side of the back is visible, it needs to be woven, too. In addition, the weft is woven in skeins, so the knots joining these skeins will need to be hidden.

Figure 6.61. Measuring the inside back height: 17 ¾ inches. Measure upward, from inside the bottom rail up to the inside of the top rail.

Photo 6.62. Measuring the lower back width (here from outside to outside): 14 inches.

BACK WARP MEASURING AND WRAPPING ON

The number of warp ends needed are:

(17¾ inches x 8) / 2 = 71

This is rounded down to 70, in order to have an even number.

The average warp end length is calculated:

Upper Length + Lower Length + 3½ inches

10½ inches + 14 inches + 3½ inches = 28 inches

Note that the 3½ inches comes from the warp wrapping around the side uprights, which are 1¾ inches thick each.

The total warp needed is (70 x 28 inches) / 36 = 55 yards.

Figure 6.63. Measuring the upper back width: 10½ inches.

The warp is measured and wound into a center-pull ball. The back is attached to the seat frame and the frame is weighted. The warp is then pegged on the lower right side.

Figure 6.64. Pegged warp.

Figure 6.65. Ten warp ends, tensioned.

Figure 6.66. Seventy warp ends, tensioned and pegged.

Figure 6.67. Seventy warp ends, front view.

Figure 6.68. Warp spaced: 35 pairs. No spacing cords are used, so as to show the beauty of the wood.

A benefit of a removable back is that it is woven off the seat frame. A dowel is tied to the bottom of the back uprights and the back is rested on a stand, for stability. The weaving is done by pulling the weft up the front side, where it is tensioned and clamped, and then weaving down the back side, and the process repeated.

The back is trapezoidal, similar to the seat, requiring the side triangles to be woven in the same way. For this chair, the number of weft picks needed to fill the triangle space at the bottom of the back is 14. This means there are 7 pairs needed for the triangle spaces. The amount of weft cord necessary to weave the triangle is estimated at 9 yards. A skein of about 14 yards is measured off, and the 9 yards for the triangle section are measured and marked with tape before being clamped to the lower rail, 1¾ inches from the left side. The remaining 5 yards are woven as part of the center section of the back. The 7 turning warps are marked, and the triangle is woven from the center section to the side upright and pegged.

Figure 6.69. Woven left side triangle (chair left, photo right).

Figure 6.70. Triangle weaving, top—turns 7, 6, and 5.

Figure 6.71. Triangle weaving, middle—turns 5, 4, and 3.

Figure 6.72. Triangle weaving, bottom—turns 3, 2, and 1.

Figure 6.73. Weft pegged to left upright.

I have made various length shed sticks and hook sticks for the wide range of bench and chair dimensions I've put together over the years. (For Fan-Back Rockers, which I no longer make, the backs have ranged up to 38 inches wide.) Weaving the chair back is easiest when the shed stick for the pattern is inserted from the top and the weft is pulled from the bottom to the top. The weft is tensioned by pulling it over the top rail and clamping it there.

Figure 6.74. Beginning the center section of the back.

Figure 6.75. Weaving the back.

The weaving pattern for the chair back is simple. Find the middle warp, which on this chair is the eighteenth warp pair. Pull the first weft pick that goes over the top rail, under the top half and over the middle warp, and then over the lower half of the back. The second pick is pulled over the top half and over the middle warp and then under the lower half. The process covers the middle warp.

A new weft skein needs to be added when the weft doesn't end in an under section of the back. The knot is the same as for a bench or chair seat and is tied to be hidden under the warp. The back picks alternate, and the knots may be under the upper or lower half of the back. Check often to be sure the picks alternate, as unweaving is not nearly as much fun as weaving.

Figure 6.76. Adding a new skein.

Figure 6.77. Weft knot hidden under the warp.

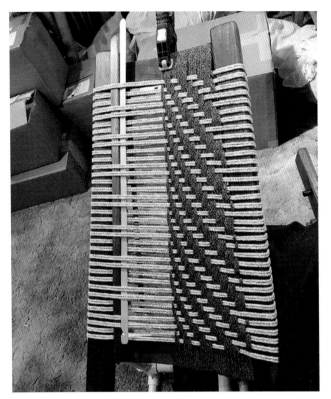

Figure 6.78. Advancing twill, halfway.

The concerns in reversing the weaving pattern are the same as for the bench and chair seat. Stay focused and keep count of the picks per shed.

Figure 6.79. Advancing twill, completed.

Figure 6.80. Back completed. *Note:* The first and last picks are the same. If they aren't, a mistake has been made.

Figure 6.81. Weft pegged on right upright.

Figure 6.82. Completed Spinner's Chair. Seat: 22″ H x 18″ D x 21″ W. Back height: 25″.

FURNITURE

As I've mentioned, there was a point in my early seat-making days when I vacillated between the worlds of chairmaking for interiors and seat making specifically for the functionality of weavers, spinners, and others whose craft and livelihood were dependent on comfortable seating.

Rocking Chairs

Once I was comfortable making benches and chairs, the next challenge was to develop a rocking chair. (Stationary chairs would evolve from my bench design.) As is so often the case, I would happen upon a better version of a rocking chair once it was tweaked to fully meet the needs of its end users.

STRAIGHT-BACK ROCKER

My first rockers were built with a fixed back. I soon discovered that weaving fixed-back chairs was awkward, so I then made the larger rockers with straight-sided, removable backs, which are easier to weave separate from the seat.

Based on my work fitting seats for weavers and spinners, I knew that the rockers needed to fit each person. One

Figure 7.1. Straight-Back Rocker; red oak; advancing 2/2 twill; weft and warp: White. Seat: 24″ W x 20″ D x 18″ H. Back: 35″ H. SPA

Figure 7.2. Straight-Back Rocker; red oak; advancing 2/2 twill; weft: Oatmeal, Warp: Dark Navy with Gold Fleck. Seat: 24″ W x 20″ D x 18″ H. Back: 35″ H. SPA

67

size doesn't fit all. The same measurements discussed in Chapter 1—seat height, depth, and width; arm height (important when reading); and back height—still applied to a rocking chair.

Next, I needed a way to cut the skids. Typically the skids on my rockers measured about 38–42 inches long, with the height of the curve measuring roughly 2–3½ inches. The plank would therefore need to be 1¾ inches thick to match the legs and back, 44 inches long, and 4 inches wide—a heavy piece that was difficult to manage at the band saw. To combat the issue of cumbersome size, I fashioned a large compass jig to cut the skids' 42-inch outer radius and the 40¼-inch inner radius, matching them to the chair legs and back.

The white version in Figure 7.1 was made in 2001 and then rewoven in 2004 with braided color cord in an oatmeal weft and navy-blue warp (Figure 7.2). I have been using this chair daily since its reweaving.

FAN-BACK ROCKER

Some of my customers requested that the rocker's back be able to tilt back farther, leading to the next design progression. The straight-back design did not fit with the splayed legs and arm support needed to support the back at the increased angle. Also, the straight-back version has its back bolted into the chair arms, while the Fan-Back Rocker has an asymmetric support bar that can be flipped over to tilt the back to 10 degrees. As it turned out, the original design with the skids cut from a large plank was a waste of lumber. Going forward, the skids for the Fan-Back Rocker would be made from 7 lamina, ¼ inch thick and 1¾ inches wide, glued up in a curved mold. The same process was used on the Knitter's Rocker, discussed in Chapter 4.

For the walnut rocker in Figure 7.3, a chocolate and beige cord was braided for the weft, and a beige and tan cord were combined for the warp. The 3/1 advancing twill weaving pattern was oriented to flow with the trapezoidal back and seat.

Figure 7.3. Fan-Back Rocker; walnut; advancing 3/1 twill; weft: Chocolate Chips, warp: Dark Nugat. Seat: 24″ W x 20″ D x 16″ H. Back: 36″ H. SPA

Figure 7.4. Fan-Back Rocker, back support bar and back angle adjuster. SPA

Figure 7.5. Fan-Back Rocker; walnut; advancing 2/2 twill; weft: Arizona Gradient; warp: Black. Seat: 24″ W x 17″ D x 17″ H. Back: 34″ H. sᴘᴀ

I continued to make and sell this design from 2007 through 2017. The customers who ordered it were a wide range of proportions, from as tall as 6 feet 8 inches to as short as 4 feet 10 inches. The fan back is a feature that lends itself to great color presentations using advancing twills (see techniques discussed in Chapter 6).

The last Fan-Back Rocker made was the Arizona Rocker in walnut (Figure 7.5). The color gradient was inspired by Arizona sunsets. While I no longer offer the Fan-Back Rocker myself due to the amount of physical effort involved in making it, this color gradient continues to be in demand and has been requested by many customers for other chairs and benches.

Side Chair

Once I became comfortable with making weaving benches, I wondered whether I might be a chairmaker, and so I started out with a Side Chair design. This process required working out the back angle in conjunction with the back leg and weaving the seat and back.

This first iteration was made for a handspinner to use at her wheel, but it was difficult for her to transport it to demonstrations and classes. (This issue is what led to the removable back solution, as discussed in Chapter 4.)

When I started braiding colored cord in early 2004, the design evolved further. Based on this design, four sets of dining room chairs were made, with the largest set being a ten-chair order.

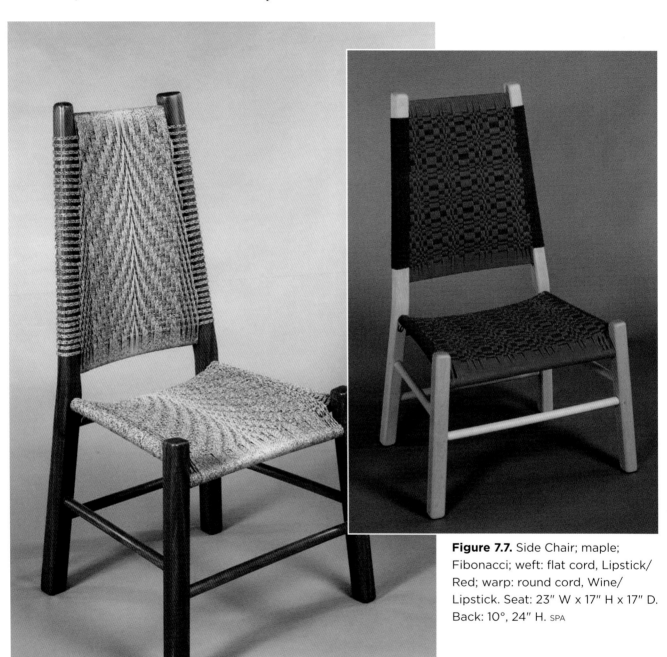

Figure 7.7. Side Chair; maple; Fibonacci; weft: flat cord, Lipstick/Red; warp: round cord, Wine/Lipstick. Seat: 23″ W x 17″ H x 17″ D. Back: 10°, 24″ H. SPA

Figure 7.6. Side Chair; walnut; 2/2 advancing twill; weft and warp: Gradient Grey. Seat: 42″ H x 20″ W x 18″ D. Seat height: 18″. SPA

Figure 7.8. Arm Chair; cherry; advancing 2/2 twill; weft and warp: Gradient Grey. 23″ W x 18″ D X 44″ H. Seat height: 18″. SPA

Settle

Further advancing the design of the Arm Chair into furniture for the living room, I developed and made a few Settles, or "two-seaters." I use the term "settle" instead of "love seat," as the piece is robust and essentially an expanded Arm Chair with six legs. I made four of these units in walnut in 2001. The original still remains in my home, and a pair were made for one customer's family room. The Settle was discontinued in 2008, when I stopped exhibiting at furniture shows. The size of the Settle made construction in my small shop a struggle and weaving a very time-intensive process. The Settle was developed before I began color braiding, and at the time only two commercial cord colors were available—white and off-white. Because of their size, these were the only pieces woven using ⅔ twills, which allowed the pattern to spread across the full width of the piece.

Desk Chair

The height of the standard desk chair is adjustable by various methods, and standard seat proportions (seat depth, seat width, back height, and arm height) still applied. The seat's arm measurements mattered, as they are typically used while the occupant is writing and reading. When used with a computer keyboard, however, the arms could be too high or too low, especially when the user is looking at a computer screen. To custom fit the seat's owner, the seat itself was fashioned based on the standard measurements (as discussed in Chapter 1), and then it was bolted to an adjustable-height swivel/tilt caster base.

The original Desk Chair had a drawback in that the arms were similar to those of rockers. As such, they could easily run into the desk drawer. In the second and subsequent Desk Chairs (Figure 7.11), I shortened the arms by 4 inches by angling the front arm support 20 degrees back.

Figure 7.9. Settle; walnut; 3/3 advancing twill; weft: Tan, warp: White. 43″ H x 53″ W x 24″ D. SPA

Figure 7.10. Desk Chair; cherry; advancing 2/2 twill; weft: Chocolate chips, warp: Light Nugat. Seat: 23″ W x 17″ D x adjustable height. Back: 24″ H; Arm: 9″ H. SPA

Figure 7.11. Desk Chair; cherry; Fibonacci; weft: Chocolate Chips, warp: Dark Nugat. Seat: 24″ W x 20″ D x adjustable height. Back: 24″ H. SPA

GALLERY

This is a collection of work starting from the early 2000s when I began braiding colored cord.

Weaver's Benches

Figure 8.1. Weaver's Bench; red oak; 2/2 diamond twill; weft: Color Wheel, warp: Black. 25″ W x 13″ D x 21″ H. SPA

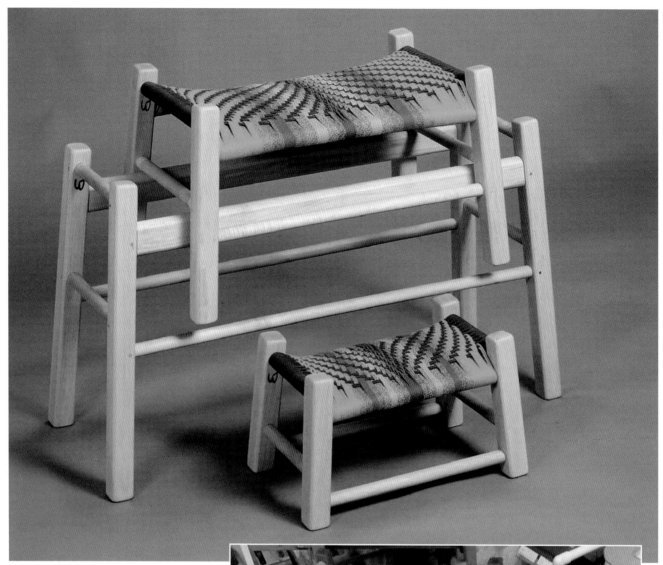

Figure 8.2. Sliding seat bench w/ footrest; maple; 2/2 undulating twill; weft: 5 Color Gradient Purple-Kelly Green, warp: Black. Seat: 24" W x 14" H x 13" D. Rails: 36" L. Total height: 30". Footrest: maple; 16" W x 9.5" H x 8" D. SPA

Figure 8.3. Weaver's Benches; white oak. Front: 2/2 undulating point twill; weft: China/Plum, warp: Gold/Natural. Back: 2/2 undulating diamond twill; weft: Gold/Natural, warp: China/Plum. 24" W x 13" D x 21" H.

Figure 8.4. Weaver's Bench w/ back; maple; 2/2 advancing point twill; weft: ⅔ China Blue, ⅓ Silver; warp: ⅔ Silver, ⅓ China Blue. Bench: 24″ W x 15″ D x 21.5″ H. Back: 18″ H.

Figure 8.5. Sliding seat Weaver's Bench (seat for Baby Wolf; on rails for Megado); maple; 2/2 advancing diamond twill; weft: Iris, warp: Navy with Gold Fleck. Seat: 24" W X 13" D x 22" H. Rails: 42" W. Total seat height: 29".

Figure 8.6. Weaver's Bench; cherry; 2/2 undulating twill; weft: Purple/Grape, warp: Plum/Mint. 22" H x 25" W x 13" D.

Figure 8.7. Weaver's Bench with back; maple; Back 2/2 advancing twill; Seat 2/2 undulating diamond twill; weft: Gradient Light Brown-Rust-Cinnamon, warp: Light Brown/Cinnamon. Bench: 28″ W x 26″ H x 15″ D. Back: 18″ H. SPA

Spinner's Chairs

Figure 8.8. Spinner's Chair; walnut; 2/2 advancing twill; weft: Rainbow, warp: Black. Seat: 18″ W x 19.5″ H x 17″ D. Back: 24″ H. SPA

Figure 8.9. Spinner's Chair with Leg Rest; walnut; weft: Arizona (Purple-Red-Orange), warp: Black. Chair: 2/2 advancing twill. Leg Rest: 2/2 advancing diamond twill. Chair: Seat: 19″ W x 19.5″ H x 16″ D. Back: 24″ H. Leg Rest: 18″ W x 16″ H x 15″ D.

Figure 8.10. Spinner's Chair with Leg Rest; cherry; weft: Gradient Silver-Copen-Deep Royal; warp: Deep Royal/ Silver. Chair: 2/2 advancing twill. Leg Rest: 2/2 advancing diamond twill. Chair seat: 20″ W x 18″ H x 16″ D. Back: 25″ H. Leg Rest: 18″ W x 16″ H x 15″ D.

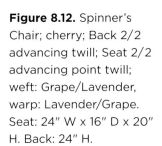

Figure 8.11. Spinner's Chair; red oak; weft and warp: Oatmeal. Seat: 2/2 advancing point twill. Back: 2/2 advancing diamond twill. Seat: 20" W x 19.5" H x 18.5" D. Back: 24" H.

Figure 8.12. Spinner's Chair; cherry; Back 2/2 advancing twill; Seat 2/2 advancing point twill; weft: Grape/Lavender, warp: Lavender/Grape. Seat: 24" W x 16" D x 20" H. Back: 24" H.

Figure 8.13. Spinner's Chair; walnut; 2/2 advancing twill; weft and warp: Jade/Duck. Seat: 24″ W x 20″ H x 16″ D. Back: 24″ H.

Figure 8.14. Spinner's Chair; cherry; 2/2 advancing point twill; weft: Dark Nugat, warp: Light Nugat. Seat: 24" W x 19.5" H x 18" D. Back: 23" H.

Figure 8.15. Spinner's Bench with back; walnut; 2/2 advancing point/ diamond twill; weft: Charcoal/Silver, warp: Silver/Charcoal. Seat: 26" W x 21" D x 23" H. Back: 25" H.

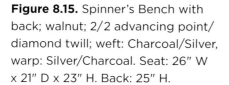

Knitter's Rockers

Figure 8.16. Knitter's Rocker; maple; 2/2 twill; weft: Black Watch, warp: Black Watch. Seat: 24″ W x 21″ D x 17.5″ H. Back: 29″ H. Skids: 40″ L. SPA

Figure 8.17. Knitter's Rocker; cherry; Back 2/2 advancing twill; Seat: 2/2 advancing diamond twill; weft: Grape/Lavender, warp: Lavender/Grape. Seat: 24″ W x 16″ D x 17″ H. Back: 24″ H. Skids: 38″ L.

Figure 8.18. Knitter's Rocker; cherry; 2/2 advancing twill; weft: Turquoise, warp: White. Seat: 22″ W x 15.5″ D x 16″ H. Back: 24″ H. Skids: 38″ L.

Fan-Back Rockers

Figure 8.19. Fan-Back Rocker; walnut; 3/1 advancing twill; weft: Chocolate Chips, warp: Dark Nugat. Seat: 42″ H x 26″ W x 40″ D. SPA

Figure 8.20. Fan-Back Rocker; walnut; 2/2 advancing twill; weft: Arizona (Purple-Red-Orange), warp: Black. Seat: 17" H x 24" W x 17" D. Back: 34" H. Skids: 40". SPA

Figure 8.21. Fan-Back Rocker; cherry; 2/2 advancing twill; weft: Dark Navy-Charcoal-Silver; warp: Dark Navy/ Charcoal. Seat: 16.5″ H x 18″ D x 21″ W. Back: 32″ H. Skids: 38″. SPA

Figure 8.22. Fan-Back Rockers; cherry; 3/1 advancing twill. SPA
His—Weft: Dark Nugat, Warp: Light Nugat. Seat: 18″ H x 18″ D x 23″ W. Back: 38″ H.
Hers—Weft: Light Nugat, Warp: Dark Nugat. Seat: 16″ H x 16″ D x 23″ W. Back: 36″ H.

Other Seating

Figure 8.23. Side Chair; walnut; advancing 2/2 twill; weft: Gradient Grey, warp: Black/Grey. Seat: 23″ W x 17″ D x 17″ H; Front: 7″ W. Back height: 24″. SPA

Figure 8.24. Arm Chair, cherry; advancing 2/2 twill; weft: Gradient Grey, warp: Black/Grey. Seat: 23″ W x 17″ D x 17″ H; Front: 7″ W. Back height: 24″. SPA

Figure 8.25. Side Chair; maple; Fibonacci pattern 1, 2, 3, 5, 3, 2, 1, 1, 2, 3, 5 in warp and weft; weft: flat cord, Reds; warp: round cord, Wine. Seat: 23″ W x 17″ D x 17″ H. Back height: 24″. SPA

Figure 8.26. Saddle Stools with removable back, cherry. Seat: advancing diamond twill; back: advancing 2/2 twill. Seat and back warp and weft: Light and Dark Lichen. Seat: 19″ D x 25.5″ H; Front: 7″ W; Back: 19″ W. Back height: 14″. Total height: 40″. SPA

Figure 8.27. Dressing Bench; cherry; Fibonacci pattern 1, 2, 3, 5, 3, 2, 1, 1, 2, 3, 5, 3 in warp and weft; weft: flat cord, Nassau Blue and Copen Blue; warp: round cord, Copen Blue and Nassau Blue. 18″ H x 15″ D x 25″ W. SPA

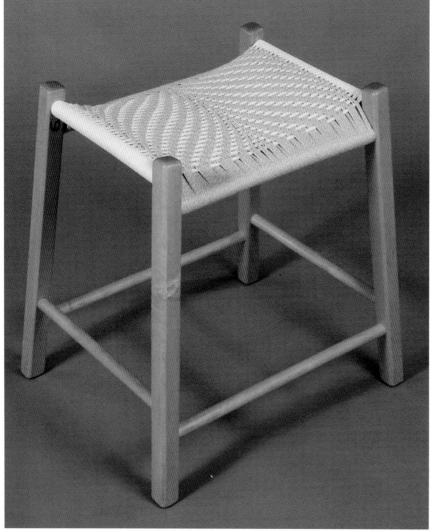

Figure 8.28. Barstool, maple; undulating 2/2 twill; weft: Dark Nugat, warp: Light Nugat. 24″ H x 20″ W x 15″ D. SPA

Figure 8.29. Desk Chair; cherry; Fibonacci pattern 1, 2, 3, 5, 3, 2, 1, 1, 2, 3, 5, 3 in warp and weft; weft: flat cord, Chocolate Chips; warp: round cord, Dark Nugat. 43″ H x 24″ W x 23″ D. SPA

APPENDIX A: CORD BRAIDING

Braided cord, or rope, has long been used in many cultures around the world. Purposes include slings to throw rocks for defense, making and adorning clothing, managing livestock, securing loads, hauling equipment, controlling sails, and the list goes on. Sizes range from surgical sutures to inches in diameter, in lengths from a few inches to thousands of yards. Fibers used in cord or rope range from natural (hemp, linen, cotton, and animal fibers) to nylon and polyester to high-tech synthetics to steel—all for specific end requirements.

There are many books available that discuss and teach the various hand-braiding methods. As I noted in the text of this book, the braided cord I started out using was natural-colored, 100 percent cotton—available at my local hardware store. Cotton was relatively easy on the hands, pliable, and inexpensive. When I began needing more than 15-yard skeins, I called the rope mill listed on the label of the cord and asked for places I could buy it in spools. (At the time, we were living in Houston, Texas.) They referred me to refinery supply houses. There I could get 1,000-yard spools of ⅛-inch cord.

After we moved to Kingsport, Tennessee, Ellen suggested I begin adding color to my weaving. After talking with a rug-weaving customer who braided her own rug warp and weft, I bought a 16-carrier braiding machine and began making cord with weaving yarns. The braider is belt-driven, and I use a variable-speed ½-horsepower motor drive. I basically learned on my own. The owner of the company that sold me my braiders helped tutor me through some steps.

Noticing that the commercial cord had a core, I then started using Maysville 8/4 carpet warp as a core. Starting with 800-yard tubes I bought at fiber shows and guild sales, I soon learned that 8-pound cones were available. Experimenting with different size cotton yarns and with the core, I found that using twenty-four threads of 8/2 cotton made a ⅛-inch cord. I also learned that there are three types of commercially available spun yarns: ring, rotor/open end, and air jet. Ring spinning machines were developed in the mid- to late 1800s to supply textile mills. Rotor/open and air jet spinning were developed in the 1970s and 1980s for faster production. Ring-spun yarns are higher twist and therefore stronger, and they can make fine/thin yarns. Rotor/open spinning produces a little softer yarn and is not capable of the very thin yarns mostly used in weaving.

Unmercerized 8/2 cottons are available in about sixty different colors. Using a single color made cord that I found "bland" or "flat," with no character. Blending two colors, however, developed visual character in woven seats. Using twenty-four threads meant that different ratios could be used for controlled blending. I found that the softer, rotor-spun yarns minimized spiral stripes in the cord.

I use two 16-carrier New England Butt Braiders to make the round cords for my benches, chairs, and stools.

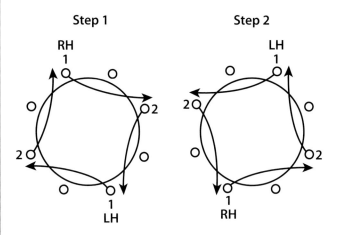

Figure A.1. Kumihimo Maru Dai 8-bobbin hollow braid. Before you begin to make a braid, space the bobbins around the Maru Dai as shown in step 1. Source: *Braids: 250 Patterns from Japan, Peru & Beyond* by Rodrick Owen (Berkeley, CA: Lacis/ Unicorn Publications, 2004), 63.

These style braiders are also called maypole braiders, referring to the maypole dance children did around the flagpole with ribbons in early May, or diamond braiders, which is the pattern seen with contrasting colors. The 16-carrier machines have the carriers paired, to make 8-bobbin braids. In Kumihimo weaving terms, the cord is an 8-bobbin hollow braid with core.

By winding 2 threads on one of the bobbin pairs and a single thread on the other, 24 threads make up the ⅛-inch cord. For a period of time, I also made ¼-inch flat braided cord on a 13-carrier braider.

Starting in 1865, New England Butt Company initially produced cast-iron butt hinges and then changed to making wire stranding and braiding machines. The company is no longer in business. However, there are many machines still in use, and new repair parts are available. Also, Wardwell Braiding currently makes braiding machines based on the New England Butt Company designs.

Figure A.2 shows the braider I purchased in 2004 and have been using since. The flat belt on the right of the machine drives eight meshed gears, which alternate gears rotating clockwise and counterclockwise. The tracks in

Figure A.2. A 16-carrier New England Butt Braider. Carriers are paired to operate as 8 bobbins. On each pair, 2 threads are wound on the lead bobbin and 1 on the trailing bobbin, for 24 threads in the cord.

Figure A.3. Shop setup of two braiders for faster production. On the left is a front feed, on the right a back feed. The flat-belt drive design is from line shaft mills, with multiple braiders on one drive shaft.

the carrier plate guide the carriers continuously, four pairs clockwise alternating with four pairs counterclockwise, doing the "maypole dance."

Typically, I braid for three to four projects ahead of the benches or chairs being made in the shop. When a customer requests two colors, I typically make the cord on one machine, first making the weft and then the warp, collecting all the cords in one thirteen-gallon, white plastic bag.

For example, using a dark blue and a light blue, I set up the braider for the weft, with 16 threads of dark blue and 8 threads of light blue—the double bobbins with a dark blue thread and a light blue thread, and the single bobbins with dark blue thread. After making the needed 200–400 yards of blended cord (depending on whether for a bench or chair, and its size), I change the single bobbins to light blue thread and continue, without cutting, to braid the warp for the remaining 100–200 yards. The bag is marked with the customer's name and colors and then stored in the studio until it's needed.

For projects like the "Arizona," "Rainbow," and "Color Wheel" that use an all-black warp, I will make about 800 yards of black cord and wind it onto a spool for storing in the studio. For popular color combinations, such as those I've named "Oatmeal" (20 Tan/4 Old Gold), "Dark Nugat" (16 Beige/8 Tan), "Light Nugat" (16 Tan/8 Beige), "Chocolate Chips" (12 Chocolate/12 Beige), or others I use in my workshops, I will also make 600–800 yards and spool them.

Bobbin Winding

A bobbin can hold about 400 yards of a single 8/2 cotton yarn, and 200 yards of a double 8/2 cotton yarn. To make 400 yards of cord, 16 double-thread bobbins and 8 single-thread bobbins are needed. Winding on a manual winder isn't practical. There are some electric bobbin winders for handloom weavers; however, I quickly burned up a used one I'd first bought. I then realized I could make a mini lathe by using a commercial sewing machine motor and electronic foot controller, with a "live" center normally used for a wood-turning lathe (Figure A.4).

Colored tape is wound around the bobbin core to help me see at a glance when a bobbin is running out as I am working in the shop. I like to use my fingers to

Figure A.4. For braider bobbins.

Figure A.5.

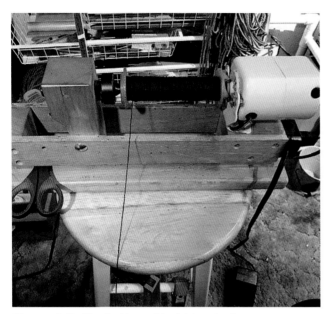

Figure A.6. Single-thread bobbin winding.

Figure A.7. Double-thread bobbin winding.

create drag while winding and to control smooth layers on the bobbins.

An 8/2 cotton yarn is 3,360 yards per pound, or 210 yards per ounce. For ease of measuring the amount of yarn wound on a bobbin, I weigh each of my bobbins on a postal scale and mark that tare weight onto each. The tare weight ranges between 1.1 ounces and 1.4 ounces, typical being 1.2 ounces. Also, I round down to 200 yards per ounce, or 20 yards per 0.1 ounce. Thus, a full bobbin is about 3.2 ounces (ranging from 3.1 ounces to 3.4 ounces total weight, depending on bobbin tare weight, or 2 ounces of yarn). For single thread, it's about 400 yards per bobbin, and for double thread about 200 yards per bobbin.

APPENDIX B:
BRAIDING GRADIENTS

2-Step Color Grading

I was inspired to make color gradients when I saw and read about Rebecca Bluestone's tapestries, which have imperceptible color gradients. Then tapestry weaver Tommie Scanlin requested a weaving bench with the color wheel in the seat. I asked her to select the particular primary colors she wanted from the UKI 8/2 unmercerized cotton color card. (These are the yarns I use to braid my color cords.) She selected the six colors shown in Figure B.1.

My goal was to create smooth transitions between two primaries. The basic process is:
- 24 threads of primary A
- 16 threads of primary A and 8 threads of primary B
- 8 threads of primary A and 16 threads of primary B
- 24 threads of primary B

Figure B.3 shows the process starting with purple.

Figure B.1. Color Wheel = six primaries. Yarns: red, orange, yellow, green, blue, purple.

Figure B.2. Weaver's Bench Color Wheel seat; red oak; straight 2/2 diamond twill on a black warp; 10 picks of each cord, splitting orange with 5 on each end, centered on blue. 25″ W x 13″ D.

Figure B.3. Here the primaries are purple, red, orange, yellow, green, and blue. There are two steps between primaries: 16 A + 8 B and then 8 A + 16 B.

Often at shows and conferences, I had people (adults and children) come into the booth, look at the bench shown in Figure B.2, and say, "Ooh, the rainbow!" Because I am a physicist, that opened up the discussion of color and the difference between pigment and light or color wheel and rainbow. After a few such discussions, a friend requested I make her a Spinner's Chair with the rainbow.

Effectively, the color wheel shown here is split between the red and purple (there is no red/purple light in the visible spectrum because red is long wavelengths and purple is short wavelengths, both just beyond what the eye can

see). Since we cannot see infrared (red) and we cannot see ultraviolet (purple), red is graded to black, and purple is graded to black (Figure B.4).

The cord is braided like the color wheel, using two steps between each of the colors, with black grading to red representing the infrared part of the spectrum, and black grading to purple representing the ultraviolet part of the spectrum.

Another way to create smooth gradients is to use the same 2-step process, only using primaries and their secondaries in the color wheel. An example is shown in Figure B.7.

Figure B.4. Rainbow/Spectrum. Yarns: black, red, orange, yellow, green, blue, purple, black.

Figure B.5. Spinner's Chair; walnut; advancing 2/2 twill; weft: Rainbow, warp: Black. Seat: 18″ W x 17″ D x 19½″ H. Back height 24″.

Figure B.6. Bench and footstool; maple; undulating 2/2 twill; Green, Jade, Blue, Special Purple, Purple. Bench seat 24″ W x 13″ D x 14″ H. Footstool 18″ W x 9″ D x 10″ H.

Figure B.7. Yarns: Purple, Special Purple, Blue, Jade, Green.

5-Step Color Grading

A good reason for using 24 threads in the braiding is that there are other convenient ratios to work with. The 5-step gradient is:

24 threads of A
20 A and 4 B
16 A and 8 B
12 A and 12 B
8 A and 16 B
4 A and 20 B
24 B

The result is a smoother transition between colors with a simpler braiding process using fewer colors. The process is illustrated in the following photos, using three colors.

Figure B.8. Dark Navy, Charcoal, and Silver.

Figure B.9.

24 Dark Navy

20 Dark Navy and 4 Charcoal

16 Dark Navy and 8 Charcoal

12 Dark Navy and 12 Charcoal

8 Dark Navy and 16 Charcoal

4 Dark Navy and 20 Charcoal

24 Charcoal

Repeat the steps from Charcoal to Silver.

The result when woven is stunning. These examples are enhanced using the advancing twill on the trapezoidal back and seat.

Figure B.10. Fan-Back Rocker; cherry; advancing 2/2 twill; Dark Navy, Charcoal, Silver 5-step gradient; 12 Dark Navy/12 Charcoal warp.

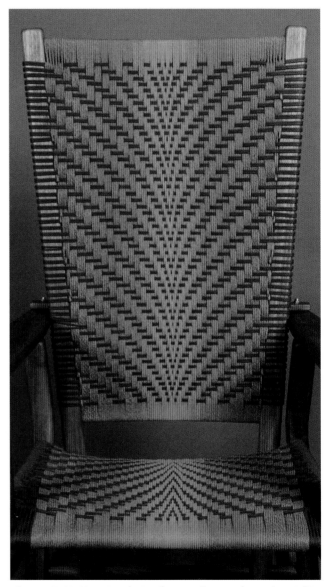

Using three colors from the color wheel creates another stunning effect.

Figure B.11. Fan-Back Rocker; walnut; advancing 2/2 twill; Arizona 5-step gradient: Purple, Red, Orange; Black warp.

These examples grade from dark to light in the center. Reversing the direction also works well.

Figure B.12. Yarns: Deep Royal, Copen, Silver.

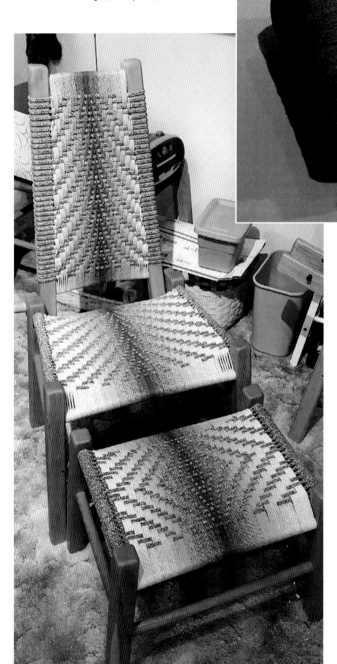

Figure B.13. Spinner's Chair and Leg Rest; cherry; Chair: advancing 2/2 twill: Leg Rest: advancing 2/2 diamond twill; 5-step gradient: Silver, Copen, Deep Royal.

Figure B.14. Leg Rest; cherry; advancing 2/2 diamond twill; 5-step gradient: Silver, Copen, Deep Royal.

APPENDIX C: WEAVING PATTERNS

I found that twill weaving patterns let me weave seat surfaces that were firm and flexible and could be visually interesting. I became excited discovering the variations possible by changing the number of picks in the sheds—a side benefit to pieces with irregular dimensions. The advancing twills could be adjusted to fit while weaving.

The three advancing twill patterns provided here are for students weaving a Weaver's Bench with seat dimensions of 24 inches wide by 13 inches deep. They are for half of a bench. Once the middle of the bench is reached, the pattern reverses.

It is left to the reader to be creative in adjusting and altering the patterns. Use the pictures of the benches, stools, and chairs throughout this book as inspiration.

For those who like traditional overshot handweaving patterns, Linda Ihle has developed a number of diamond patterns for Weaver's Benches and Dressing Benches. In 2017, she attended the Weave-a-Bench workshop at the MidAtlantic Fiber Association (MAFA) conference. When she returned home, she took things further by reweaving her workshop bench—correcting a couple of errors—and making a couple more benches for her studio. Linda liked overshot patterns and developed a number of diamond patterns for benches using computer software. These patterns are specifically for 24-inch wide by 13-inch deep Weaver's Benches and 20-inch wide by 15-inch deep Dressing Benches. Students in subsequent workshops have used Linda's patterns with her permission.

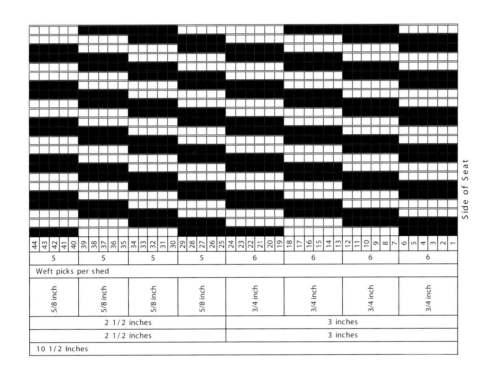

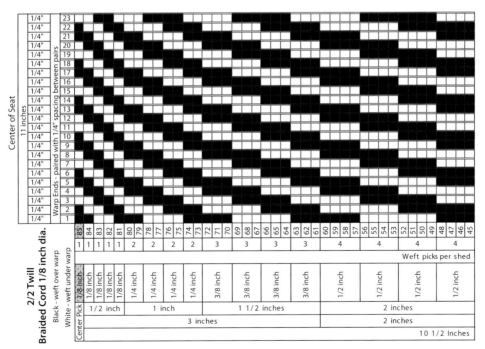

Figure C.1. Advancing twill.

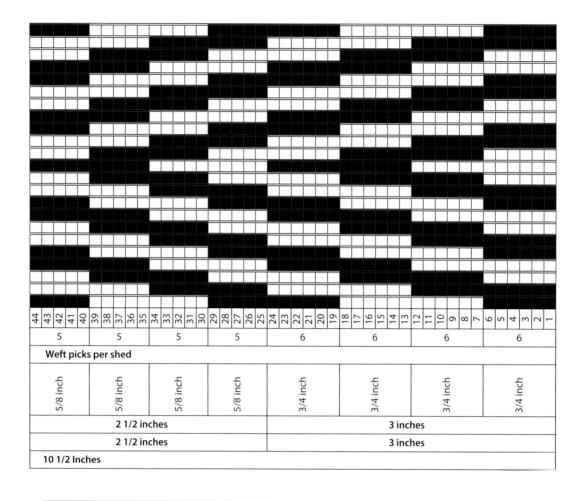

Figure C.2. Advancing point twill.

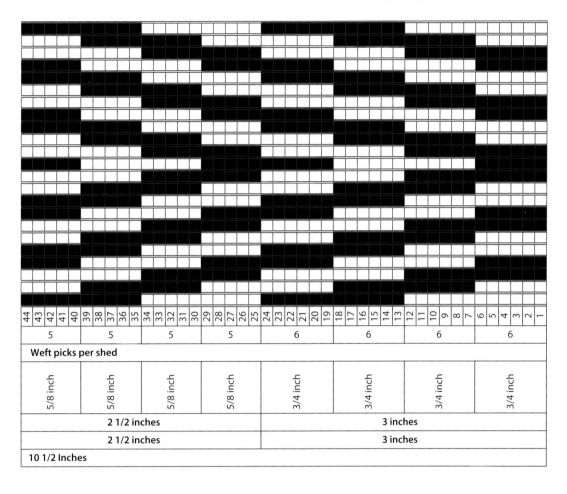

44 43 42 41 40	39 38 37 36 35	34 33 32 31 30	29 28 27 26 25	24 23 22 21 20 19	18 17 16 15 14 13	12 11 10 9 8 7	6 5 4 3 2 1
5	5	5	5	6	6	6	6

Weft picks per shed

5/8 inch	5/8 inch	5/8 inch	5/8 inch	3/4 inch	3/4 inch	3/4 inch	3/4 inch

2 1/2 inches				3 inches			

2 1/2 inches				3 inches			

10 1/2 Inches							

Figure C.3. Advancing diamond twill.

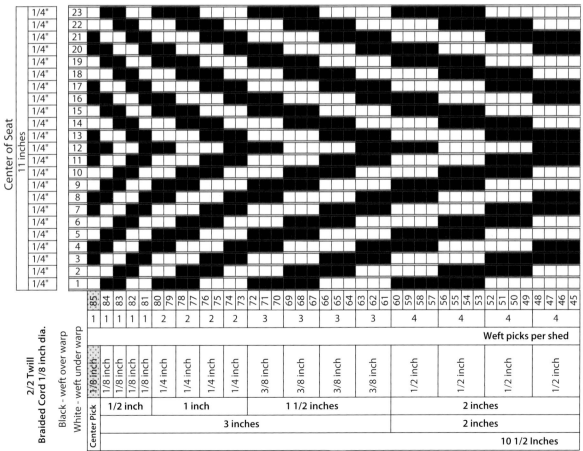

Center of Seat
11 inches

2/2 Twill
Braided Cord 1/8 inch dia.

Black - weft over warp
White - weft under warp

1/4"	23
1/4"	22
1/4"	21
1/4"	20
1/4"	19
1/4"	18
1/4"	17
1/4"	16
1/4"	15
1/4"	14
1/4"	13
1/4"	12
1/4"	11
1/4"	10
1/4"	9
1/4"	8
1/4"	7
1/4"	6
1/4"	5
1/4"	4
1/4"	3
1/4"	2
1/4"	1

Center Pick	85	84 83 82 81	80 79	78 77 76 75 74 73	72 71 70 69	68 67 66 65 64 63	62 61 60 59 58 57	56 55 54 53	52 51 50 49	48 47 46 45
	1	1 1 1 1	2 2	2 2	3	3	3	4	4	4	4

Weft picks per shed

Center Pick	1/8 inch	1/8 inch	1/8 inch	1/8 inch	1/4 inch	1/4 inch	1/4 inch	1/4 inch	3/8 inch	3/8 inch	3/8 inch	3/8 inch	1/2 inch	1/2 inch	1/2 inch	1/2 inch

1/2 inch	1 inch	1 1/2 inches	2 inches

3 inches			2 inches

10 1/2 Inches			

Diamond Twill Patterns by Linda Ihle

Figure C.4. 8 Diamond for Dressing Bench.

Figure C.5. 3 Diamond for Dressing Bench.

43
42
41
40
39
38
37
36
35
34
33
32
31
30
29
28
27
26
25
24
23
22
21
20
19
18
17
16
15
14
13
12
11
10
9
8
7
6
5
4
3
2
1

Notice line 22 is different
between version 1 and 2

1 2 3 4 5 6 7 8 9 10 11 12 13 14 15 16 17 18 19 20 21 22 23

Figure C.6. Offset Diamond #1 for Weaver's Bench.

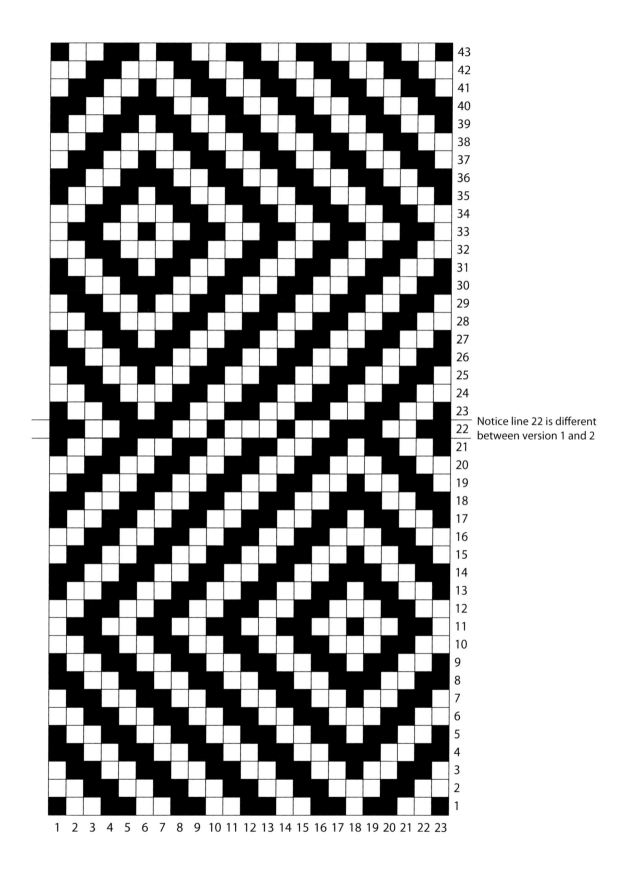

43
42
41
40
39
38
37
36
35
34
33
32
31
30
29
28
27
26
25
24
23
22 — Notice line 22 is different
21   between version 1 and 2
20
19
18
17
16
15
14
13
12
11
10
9
8
7
6
5
4
3
2
1

1 2 3 4 5 6 7 8 9 10 11 12 13 14 15 16 17 18 19 20 21 22 23

Figure C.7. Offset Diamond #2 for Weaver's Bench.

Figure C.8. Multi Diamond for Weaver's Bench.

Figure C.9. Multi Diamond #1 for Dressing Bench.

Figure C.10. Offset Multi Diamond for Dressing Bench.

Figure C.11. Offset Diamond for Dressing Bench.

GLOSSARY

Brad. A thin, wire nail with a barrel-shaped head.

Braid. General class of interlacing threads, yarns, or other fibers to make cord or rope.

Braider. A powered machine to consistently make long lengths of cord and rope, typically in a simple maypole style.

Chamfer. A bevel, or a narrow, flat edge along two right-angled surfaces; seen also on the starting flat edge of the legs when shaping their tops and bottoms.

Cord cutter. A safety box cutter used to easily cut cord (safer than a knife, easier than scissors).

Drawdown. A graphic representation of weft and warp interlacements used to create a woven piece; also called a pattern.

Heddle hook. A short hook, traditionally metal but also available in plastic and other flexible materials, typically with a handle, used by handweavers to pull warp threads through heddles on looms; a short metal hook with a handle used to pull cord through attachment holes on seat rails; a short metal hook with a handle used to weave the last 2–3 inches of a seat or back.

Hook stick. A flat tool (usually wood in the case of weaving) with hooks on one or both ends used to pull/draw the weft through the warp shed.

Mortise. A circular or rectangular hole cut into wood and sized to receive a corresponding part, the tenon, which together lock or secure a joint or two pieces (commonly used by woodworkers for thousands of years).

Peg. A wood dowel with a slightly tapered end used to strengthen mortise and tenon joints; a poplar, ¼-inch-diameter dowel trimmed to a wedge, usually ⅞-inch long, driven in to wedge cord into attachment holes in rails and chair backs.

Pick. One weft cord woven through a warp shed.

Rails. The horizontal bars of a seat, and the top and bottom of a chair back, mortised into the chair back uprights.

Shed. The temporary separation of the warp cords into upper and lower gaps in order to easily weave the weft.

Shed stick. A flat tool (usually wood) used in weaving to hold open (or to close) the shed.

Spacing cord. Cord wrapped around the side rails to keep the warp spaced.

Splay. The outward angle of the bench, stool, and chair legs and back when looking at the chair from the front.

Stretchers. Dowels spaced lower than the seat rails to maintain leg spacing and make the bench, stool, or chair frame rigid.

Tenon. The end of a wood piece measured and cut to be inserted in a coordinating mortise, together making a secure joint; here, the ends of rails, stretchers, and back rails that are shaped to fit into round or rectangular mortises.

Warp. The tightly stretched longitudinal threads that hold the tension of the weaving on weaving looms; here, they are wrapped side to side on the seat rails and side to side around the back uprights.

Weft. Cord (or thread) woven crosswise, over and under the warp cords.

Witness mark. Used for matching the legs after initial cutting; used to mark front leg pairs, back leg pairs, and side leg pairs to properly cut the 5-degree compound angles on the legs and drill the mortises in the legs.

CONTRIBUTORS

Jeffery C. Sturgill

Sturgill Photographic Arts (SPA)

Kingsport, Tennessee

Jeff has been a professional photographer for more than forty years after getting his bachelor's degree in fine art photography. His interest in photography began in childhood.

His work has been published in *Sports Illustrated*, *Time* magazine, *Country Living*, *MD News*, and numerous brochures and publications. During the two decades Jeff and Walt have known each other, Jeff has been the exclusive studio photographer of Walt's work.

Brandy Clements

Silver River Center for Chair Caning (SRCCC)

Asheville, North Carolina

Brandy is a fourth-generation chair caner and co-owner of Silver River Center for Chair Caning. After a decade restoring thousands of chairs, she and her husband, Dave Klingler, opened Silver River Center for Chair Caning to create a new generation of chair weavers and to cultivate a reverence for the ancient and global tradition. The nation's only chair caning school and museum provides opportunities for hands-on weaving and imparting contemporary/historical information to visitors. Brandy and Dave are dedicated to the preservation of the craft through education, restoration, and travel.

Brandy has traveled extensively to study chairs throughout the United States and in England and Scotland. SRCCC is an Official Education Center of the Southern Highland Craft Guild. Brandy and Dave teach regularly in the school, online, and on location at esteemed venues including Arrowmont School of Arts and Crafts, Penland School of Craft, and John C. Campbell Folk School. They have been featured in *American Craft* magazine and *USA Today*, as well as on PBS.

Linda Ihle

Kill Devil Hills, North Carolina

Linda's interest in weaving began as a child when she was given her first 2-shaft table loom. Summertime trips through the Amish country to get to family on the East Coast introduced Linda to large floor looms and the fabrics made with them. In 2009, Linda joined a local fiber guild, where she was reintroduced to weaving, thus beginning her real weaving journey.

Linda hosts weaving, sewing, and dyeing workshops near her home, with instructors such as Kathrin Weber and Daryl Lancaster. Her weaving interests include mixing dyed warps and weaving twill, rep, and plain weave on her 4- and 8-shaft looms. She enjoys the design process of weaving and dressing the loom as much as (or more than) actually weaving the fabric. She has dabbled in spinning, knitting, and wet felting, but weaving is her real passion.

Linda designs house plans using CAD software. After taking a bench-weaving workshop with Walt at a MAFA conference, she decided to play with the diamond draft Walt had supplied. She created the diamond twill patterns included in this book.

ABOUT THE AUTHORS

JAY PULLI

Walter Turpening

I grew up in southeastern Michigan, graduated from high school, and received degrees in physics and geology/geophysics. I joined Gulf Oil in 1972 and worked in geophysics research, development, and technology support for Gulf, Sohio/BP; then I started Reservoir Imaging, Inc.

Ellen and I married in 1977. We lived in Texas and Pennsylvania. In 1997, Ellen didn't want to live in Houston anymore, and when she found a clinical dietitian position in Kingsport, Tennessee, we moved in 1998. I decided to become a chairmaker and set up a small shop. In July 1998, I did my first national show at the Handweavers Guild of America Convergence in Atlanta, Georgia.

For nearly twenty years, woodworking was a hobby. While working to make a comfortable footstool, we took a vacation to the Southern Appalachians, where I saw Shaker and rush-woven chairs and benches. Returning to Houston, I began teaching myself how to weave curved seat surfaces. Ellen was a weaver and taught me various weaving patterns and provided help with color blending.

Since 1998 I have been making benches, stools, and chairs full time. Starting with simple benches custom fitted to the weaver at their loom, things evolved into barstools, spinner's chairs, dining chairs, and so on. Once I felt I was a chairmaker, I made a rocking chair. All in all, twenty or so design variations have been developed. I have taken the advice of a professional woodworker: "As you get older, make lighter things." Since 2017 I have trimmed offerings to more fiber arts benches, stools, and chairs.

One lesson learned early in the O&G years: "Retirement can be a bad thing . . . I witnessed too many retiring to nothing but travel, golf, fishing . . . and dying in three to five years. I removed the retirement concept from my attitude. I changed careers."

DEBORAH HELD

Deborah Held

Debbie Held is a freelance writer and international fiber arts educator. She's a recurring contributor to *Spin Off* magazine and its blog *PLY*, tinyStudio *Creative Life* magazine, the SweetGeorgia blog, and more, and she's the writer behind the Interweave column, "Her Handspun Habit." A truly contented spinster, Debbie lives on an urban farm in Atlanta, Georgia, with an enormous Persian cat named Stanley. Both enjoy watching the spinner's flock of Shetland sheep living in the yard below their windows. Write to them (all) at www.debbieheld.com.